Truth and Meaning in Political Science

MERRILL POLITICAL SCIENCE SERIES

Under the Editorship of

John C. Wahlke

Department of Political Science
The University of Iowa

Truth and Meaning in Political Science

An Introduction to Political Inquiry

MARIA J. FALCO

Le Moyne College

Charles E. Merrill Publishing Company
A Bell & Howell Company
Columbus, Ohio 43216

Published by
Charles E. Merrill Publishing Company
A Bell & Howell Company
Columbus, Ohio 43216

ISBN: 0-675-08934-4

Library of Congress Catalog Card Number: 73-75328

1   2   3   4   5   6   7   8   9—79   78   77   76   75   74   73

Printed in the United States of America

To Eli and all his minions

Acknowledgments

The influence, ideas, inspiration and guidance of a great many persons went into the writing of this book, some direct and indirect, some conscious and unconscious, some as far back as graduate school and my post-doctoral experiences at Yale, and some as recent as yesterday's class. Those more immediately and directly involved with the actual production of the manuscript, however, include Professor John Wahlke, whose encouragement and evaluations of the outline and manuscript were enormously helpful and without whose enthusiasm for the project in the first place, this book might never have been written; Father Thomas J. Kent, S. J., of the philosophy department of Le Moyne College, whose comments and criticisms caused me to re-think and re-write whole segments of the chapter on values; Father Thomas Murray, S. J., of the physics department at Le Moyne, who offered some interesting phraseology for the glossary; the Faculty Research Committee of Le Moyne College which granted me the sabbatical allowing me the time to complete the manuscript; Mr. Roger Ratliff and Ms. Susan Ziegler of the Charles E. Merrill Publishing Company, whose practical and editorial assistance were essential to the entire enterprise; and Mrs. Connie Hall, who was good enough to type the manuscript in her spare time and who managed to meet most deadlines despite some rather trying circumstances.

I am also deeply indebted to Professor David Easton for permission to quote extensively from two of his articles on recent developments in political science, and to the Princeton University Press for their permission to quote from Arnold Brecht's *Political Theory: The Foundations of Twentieth Century Political Thought.*

Contents

CHAPTER I

Some Basic Questions

The major premise upon which this book is based is that political science is a social science discipline. Just a few years ago such a statement would have been considered highly controversial, and in some circles today it might still be considered a matter of some dispute. But for the great majority of persons who call themselves political scientists it is just a statement of fact. The reason is that the research techniques and methods of the social sciences and the rationale or logic behind those methods have been largely accepted as the proper mode of procedure for scholarly research in political science. Previously, the techniques of other disciplines from which political science originally evolved (history, law, philosophy) dominated the field. Today political scientists look primarily to sociologists, psychologists, economists, anthropologists—other social scientists—both for insights into ways to approach their own discipline, and for methods of ferreting out the significant information from which general concepts and theories concerning political behavior, whether individual, societal or international, can be built. All of this is the result of what has been called the "behavioral revolution" in political science—the deflection of political science away from the consciously or unconsciously normative, deductive, or purely empirical concerns of philosophy, law, and history, and toward the consciously and deliberately non-

1

normative, theoretical, and rigorously methodological orientations of science and the social sciences. The change has been a rather traumatic one for political science, and approval of it is as yet by no means universal. But its occurrence is no longer in dispute.

The reasons for this revolution will be presented later in this book, when a brief history of the discipline will be essayed. Several more preliminary questions must be grappled with first, however, from the point of view of the newly initiated political scientist, the undergraduate student. Some of the questions which we will attempt to answer here are: What is social science research methodology? How is it different from what other disciplines call research? Why should undergraduate students of political science be required to study it?

First of all, let us return to our opening statement: political science is a social science discipline. Briefly, this means that the political scientist studies those aspects of human individual and social behavior which impinge, directly or indirectly, upon the political arena. The other social sciences—sociology, anthropology, economics and psychology—study different aspects of the same phenomenon, human behavior. Psychologists are mainly concerned with individuals, how they learn, how their personalities develop, what factors (genetic and physiological makeups, family and social environments) influence that development, and what cumulative effects similar patterns of development might have when individuals are combined in groups. Sociology primarily studies men in large and small groups, acting and interacting in various roles and on different levels (strata) within and between groups. Anthropologists study what have been called "primitive"—that is, presumably simple (preindustrial, tribal, etc.)—societies as well as complex ones, in an attempt to reveal the bases for human social interaction in their purest form. They delineate and distinguish patterns of different cultural orientations of human life as they exist in different societies, search for cross-cultural similarities and evolutionary trends, and attempt to predict how change and development from so-called simple to so-called complex forms may take place. Economists, like political scientists in the political arena, study human individual and social behavior, and as much of it as may relate to the market place.

What distinguishes the social sciences from other socially related disciplines like history, law, and philosophy, aside from specific subject matters, is primarily the rationales behind their research methodologies. History studies past human behavior, but it assumes that such behavior is unique, that events of the past are best understood in their original contexts, and therefore, being unique, all attempts to formulate generalizations from them about similar events (political or otherwise) at different times and places are futile. In other words, history is basically empirical, factual and, as far as most historians are concerned, nontheoretical.

Law is basically a moralistic and deductive discipline. Certain norms for individual and corporate behavior are laid down by authoritative lawgivers or by revered customs, and students of the law apply these norms to specific situations in an attempt to discover the consequences. To be "legalistic" means to interpret these norms narrowly and without much thought to "extenuating circumstances"—i.e., to be purely deductive in method. Not all lawyers, judges, law enforcement officers, and students of law are so rigidly legalistic as to deny the importance of such circumstances (including what is sometimes euphemistically called "politics"), but the basic technique for determining what will in all likelihood be considered legal or illegal behavior in any situation is deduction—the logic of the law. The law itself may eventually be altered by an accumulation of such circumstances as may reveal it to be seriously defective or in need of change (what Oliver Wendell Holmes, Jr. called "experience"), but the method which determines the application of the law, unless indeed altered by those same lawgivers (Congress, the courts, etc.) or customs-arbiters (the influence of television on presidential nominating conventions, for example), is still basically deduction: tell me (the jury) what the law is, and what it was that you did, and I shall tell you whether you acted legally or not (guilty or not guilty).

Philosophy is traditionally also normative and deductive in orientation, concerned with explaining reality, the world as man can know it, and all aspects of truth and meaning. Many of today's philosophers still consider their discipline to be normative and deductive; that is, they believe their main goal is to help men to live their lives in a meaningful way through the pursuit of wisdom. They posit certain "truths" about human nature and objective reality, and through considerable effort to clarify and understand these truths, they attempt to derive from them certain guidelines or even moral imperatives for daily humanistic living.

Another school of philosophy has arisen in recent years, however, which would question the validity of this entire enterprise. To the positivistic or analytic philosopher, philosophy is no longer concerned with deducing guidelines for action or moral imperatives from "self-evident" truths. Its main purpose, as they see it, is to clarify the meaning of language, the principal tool by which human beings learn about things and how to adapt to their surroundings. As an adjunct to science, its *modus operandi* is not to assume certain things to be true, but to make it possible for the scientist to discover what is true, by clarifying and explicating the uses of language in the discovery process and in the procedures by which truth is demonstrated and knowledge validated. Positivistic philosophy does not produce a roster of guides to "good" or humanistic living, but rather a series of statements about reality which can be reasonably accepted as true because of the process by which they were unfolded. The acceptance of these truths and the actions which may or may not follow from them are held to depend in large measure upon the degree to which the individuals or societies which apprehend them are in fact ready to accept and act upon them. Philosophy can clarify meaning and help reveal truth, but it cannot claim that any course of action by other human beings or societies must necessarily or morally follow.

Thus while philosophy, as the positivists see it, may still continue to be logical or deductive in the technique by which it validates statements about reality, it must also be empirical in the ways in which it rallies the evidence necessary to construct those statements, and its aim is no longer a normative one (telling people or societies what they "should" do). It holds instead that there is no logical connection between a normative statement (what "ought" to be) or value judgment (a choice or a statement of interest, need or emotional preference) and a factual statement; the former cannot be derived from the latter, and therefore the two orders of statements should be kept separate and not be confused. It is this orientation toward reality, the orientation of the analytic philosopher, which is the basis of all social science, and indeed, all scientific research.

Undeniably, this positivistic or scientific orientation of the "new" philosophy is a serious break with the moralistic endeavors of the old (the search for the "good life"). And indeed many would relegate it to a separate category of intellectual inquiry, calling it not philosophy per se but the "philosophy of science" or of "social science," thus labeling it for what it "really is"—a pseudo-philosophy. To people of this persuasion, the role of philosophy proper is what it has always been—to guide men through the quagmires and labyrinths of everyday life, with rational insights into those types of conduct which will best insure the realization of peace and harmony with oneself and one's fellow men. To this the analytic philosopher is likely to reply: What you really want to study is not so much philosophy as psychology—not how one "should" behave, but why one behaves as one does, and how stability or harmony can be attained in human social interactions. The enterprise which the normative philosopher calls philosophy is futile and empty, they say. Value judgments or moral imperatives cannot be derived from "self-evident" or any other kind of truth; truths are not self-evident but must be verified by actual empirical evidence or validated by logic. To hold anything else is to be self-deceptive and to adhere to an illusory concept of truth. And so the argument goes on—each calling the other names and denying each other the right to call itself "philosophy." More of this dispute and its effect on political science will be presented later.

In actual fact, the scientist, like the analytic philosopher, holds that all generalizations about reality in science, whether arrived at by intuition or by careful weighing and measuring of empirical evidence, must be tested and validated in the real world, empirically as well as logically, and cannot logically be assumed to have any moral, ethical or otherwise normative implications for human or other behavior. (The Bubonic Plague, for example, was not God's judgment upon the "evil ways" of fourteenth century Europe.) Thus the belief that "what is, should be" has no standing in the world of science and holds no meaning for the sciences of human behavior. Only statements about "what is" are probed; "what should be" is left to the metaphysician, the normative social or political "philosopher" (or ethician and policy theorist), and eventually the politician, to determine.

The scientist leaves normative considerations or value judgments to these others primarily because the solutions and patterns of choices which they involve are rooted in the specific cultural orientations and preferences of that society which discusses and grapples with them, while his own scientific—i.e., empirical and logical—statements about reality can be demonstrated to be applicable everywhere, or almost everywhere. (For example: "In democracies it is believed that governments should behave in accordance with the wishes of the governed." Not: "Government should behave in accordance with the wishes of the governed." The first is or may be an empirical finding of fact; the second is a value judgment.) Or so the theory goes. Rightly or wrongly, it is this rationale which is the foundation of present-day social science research and therefore of contemporary political inquiry.

This does not mean that the political scientist divorces himself completely from questions of political policy or suppresses his critical faculties on matters of current political concern. On these issues he is as much a citizen of his society and an assessor of its values and their implementation as is any other member of that society. He does not cease to be a citizen because he is a social scientist. What it does mean is that as a political scientist, in his professional capacity as a member of the social science community, and while performing his role as an investigator of human political behavior, the statements he makes about politics and the political arena will be empirical, factual, theoretical and logical only. When he does engage in normative judgments, it is to be expected that he will probably be better informed than the rank-and-file member of his political community, but his values, formed as much by that society as are those of his fellow citizens, will probably be as conflicting and/or contradictory as theirs. (For example, he may find himself attempting to reconcile both a desire for lower taxes and a need for better educational facilities in his community. Which will receive priority in his own mind will depend upon the peculiar set of circumstances in which he finds himself—his income, the number of children he has, etc.—and his own assessment of the greater of his and/or his community's two needs.)

Thus the scientist pursues certitude (although he may never attain it) through the application of the scientific method (the logic of scientific inquiry) to his particular subject for investigation. It is the only way he knows to assure reliability and validity in the observations and generalizations he makes about his subject. For it is only by the faithful application of the canons of scientific methodology that he can hope to attain a degree of impartiality and objectivity, or secure an unbiased conclusion to his research efforts. This is the goal of the scientist, but it is not necessarily that of the citizen-participant. The citizen very often argues from a particular viewpoint and attempts to achieve particular goals through his participation in the political process. He is frequently biased, on his own or his community's behalf, and may proceed in a biased and sometimes even polemical manner.

The scientist, on the other hand, seeks only one goal through the process of scientific research—the attainment of as high a degree of truth as is humanly possible. He is a discoverer, not an advocate; an explorer of the unknown, not a revealer of dogma; a skeptic, not an authority. His guiding principle, if you will, is "Method," not "The Good," and his major instrument for achieving his goal is

"Technique," not "The Right" (or law: Recht, Droit, etc.). He is completely earthbound and empirical, not transcendental and mystical. But, being human, he can also aspire and dream. The fruits of his imaginings, however, must be tested and probed, and somehow verified empirically and validated logically if they are to remain within the realm of the scientific enterprise.

It is this reliance on method, and the truth which it is presumed to effect, which distinguishes the scientist from the citizen. The scientist seeks "the truth" as he can know it; the citizen seeks "the good" for himself and/or his community, as he sees it. The two may be, and frequently are, related—that is, what the citizen thinks is true influences what he believes to be good or in his own interest. But the scientist is required to validate his truth claims and knows that he can draw no logical conclusions about what ought to follow from them, while the citizen is seldom in a position to validate his truth claims but he is almost always obliged to make a determination on what should follow from them. The student of political science can and probably will take on both roles, if he wishes, but he should be able to distinguish the two, and to understand the responsibilities and hazards incumbent upon them both. It is the role and rationale of the scientist to which the student is specifically socialized when he becomes a social scientist. The other he attains by reason of his citizenship and the process by which he was, and continues to be, socialized into his civil society.

It is because political science originated in the tradition of the early political philosophers (Plato, Aristotle, etc.) and only recently came to be initiated into the discipline of science that the confusion between the two roles continues to exist. In fact the early history of American political science is replete with declarations that the purpose of the discipline was "citizenship education." It was assumed that the political scientist was actually a student of the norms and values which reason dictated were the attributes of the "good state," in an absolute sense. While the normative political philosopher or occasional policy scientist may today continue to do so, the political scientist as a social scientist does not. This is because he has come to see reason (as in "Right Reason") not as an absolute standard which men attempt to perceive, but as a tool of the mind, a neutral method, logic. As such, therefore, it cannot dictate or reveal any "right" way to do things; it can only attempt to indicate the truth about things.

It is this change in outlook which distinguishes the attitude of the Enlightenment from that of the present—the beliefs of the authors of the Declaration of Independence from those of modern political scientists. And it is basically the reason why we can no longer view statements like "All men are created equal" as undisputed statements of fact ("We hold these truths to be self-evident"), from which certain action imperatives can be deduced ("That whenever any form of government becomes destructive of these ends, it is the right of the people to alter or abolish it"). Instead, they are the values which those men who claim to aspire to democratic government may hold. All of this will be further explained later. But meanwhile, the student of political science is expected to study, understand, and utilize the scientific method and rationale in his own neophyte attempts to do political science research, and for several very important reasons.

First of all, the scientific method is the accepted rationale for inquiry in this discipline, and because this rationale is the same as that applied in science in general as well as in other social sciences, it is likely to endure for some time to come. It would therefore be highly illogical for the student to ignore it or refuse to study it if he intends to consider himself a student of political science.

Second, the substantive aspects of his discipline, the actual subject matter which he studies daily in his different courses, change constantly as this very research continues throughout the discipline and throughout the world. Since all education aims to prepare the student for the long-range rather than for the merely immediate future, it is the better part of wisdom to enable him to discern for himself the transitory from what is likely to endure. If he understands the method by which present "knowledge" is arrived at, he can better adapt himself to new "knowledge" when it is attained, and perhaps even participate in the obtaining of some of that knowledge on his own.

Third, even should he not decide to become a professional political scientist by continuing his studies in graduate school, the training he receives in distinguishing fact from opinion, evidence from inference, correlation from cause, probability from providence, ideology from utopia, will stand him in good stead in whatever line of endeavor he eventually chooses. For it is the ability to think in a disciplined and logical manner and to rally one's facts in an unbiased fashion which distinguishes the moderate man from the demagogue, the man of reason from the brute. In a world of overheated emotions, such a technique can be much valued and indeed indispensable for the survival of civilization. Thus while values themselves may be held in abeyance throughout scientific inquiry and discourse, these very techniques may in fact be essential for the preservation and/or attainment of certain values. The citizen may find it to his extraordinary advantage to have some knowledge of the scientific "ethic." We will return to this point at the end of this introduction to political inquiry.

The purpose of this book, therefore, is to orient the beginning student of political science to the rationale or "logic" of research methodology which lies at the foundation of his and all other scientific disciplines, and to make him cognizant of some of the major disputes and problems which face all scientists so engaged, particularly political scientists. The subject matter of this book can be found in greater depth and at more difficult levels of discourse in many diversely titled tomes, some of which designate themselves as coming under the classification of the philosophy of science or of social science, of the scope and methods of political science, of political analysis, of political or social inquiry, and more recently, of "metapolitics." Whatever the title, the topic is that of the problem of truth and meaning in the social sciences, and in political science in particular.

It is this field which we endeavor to lay bare before the beginning student, in what we hope is a simple, yet comprehensive manner. Where "jargon" or difficult language seems unavoidable it will be used, but a glossary has been provided at the end of the book for instant reference. An extensive bibliography and suggested reading lists at the end of each chapter have also been included for the student who wishes to read further.

The book is organized in the following manner:

Chapter two will show the interrelationships which exist between culture, philosophy as traditionally conceived, and science, and will attempt a brief overview of the development of science and the philosophy of science as we presently know them.

Chapter three will delve into the problem of epistemology or how we know what we know. It will outline a history of the development of knowledge theory and will bring us to the foundation of modern research methodology or "scientific method."

Chapter four will explain what is meant by the "scientific method" and how it is applied in the social sciences and political science in particular.

Chapter five will show the role of mathematics and measurement, statistics and probability theory in present-day science, and why political science research now seems so much wedded to mathematical formulations.

Chapter six will undertake a brief history of political science as an academic discipline and will attempt to explain the growth of the behavioral movement of the 1950s and 1960s, and the development of the present split which exists between the behavioral "establishment" and those who would change the course of the discipline by orienting it toward a greater concern for social and political values.

Chapter seven will attempt to assess the role of value theory in political science and its relationship to the growing concerns of the policy theorists—social and political—who are pressing so strenuously to be heard by the entire social science as well as the political science community.

Finally, a brief concluding chapter will sum up some of the major controversies of the book, show how they are intertwined, and indicate, hopefully without too much repetition, what alternative paths for their solution appear to be open to the future political scientist.

Suggested Readings

Eulau, Heinz, and James G. March, eds. *Political Science: The Behavioral and Social Sciences Survey, Political Science Panel.* Englewood Cliffs, N. J.: Prentice-Hall, A Spectrum Book, 1969.

Homans, George C. *The Nature of Social Science.* New York: Harcourt, Brace and World, 1967.

Lasswell, Harold D. *The Future of Political Science.* New York: Prentice-Hall, Atherton Press, 1963.

Lipset, Seymour Martin, ed. *Politics and the Social Sciences.* New York: Oxford University Press, 1969.

Somit, Albert and Joseph Tanenhaus. *American Political Science: A Profile of a Discipline.* New York: Prentice-Hall, Atherton Press, 1964.

CHAPTER II

Culture, Philosophy, and Science

Culture, as defined by anthropologists,[1] consists of those patterns of beliefs, norms and values which the members of a particular group or subgroup come to share by reason of their common everyday experiences and interactions with their environment and with each other.

Philosophy in the traditional, not analytical, sense is a rationalizing and ordering of those beliefs, values, and norms, or portions of them, into a consistent overall pattern or world-view (*weltanschauung*).[2] This general view of reality is then used as a basis from which specific notions of what is proper or improper to believe, do, or value in specific instances in everyday life may be derived. In other words, culture provides the data for philosophy as traditionally conceived, and traditional philosophy provides the guidelines for the further development of culture.

Science is sometimes viewed as a particular subculture—those patterns of beliefs, norms, and values shared by a particular subgroup of individuals who call themselves scientists. What is different about science and scientists is that persons who call

---

1. A. L. Kroeber and Clyde Kluckhohn, *Culture* (New York: Vintage Books, 1963).
2. See Abraham Kaplan's "Introduction" to *The New World of Philosophy* (New York: Vintage Books, 1961).

themselves scientists and share the vocation of science are frequently participants in two separate but not necessarily conflicting types of cultures. Such a situation is not unique by any means. Persons who originate in one culture and emigrate to another but settle themselves into specific enclaves (or ghettos) within the host country are in a similar situation. What is unique about science is that the individual, in taking on the identity of the scientist, is not in any sense required to renounce his previous allegiances and mode of life. Science is the one culture which most of the nations of the world today encourage their own members to foster and espouse.

The reason for this is that science is considered to be a culture which does not necessarily conflict with or endanger the host culture, and which, on the contrary, can bring great benefits to the host and its adherents. Occasionally there may be some popular disaffection over some of the technological outputs of the scientific culture (all-digit dialing, know-all computer data banks, etc.) but, on the whole, science is believed to be a tool which the host culture can use to its own advantage, rather than a rival which might endanger it and therefore require it to expend great amounts of energy defending its superiority. In other words, very little sense of competition exists between national cultures and science, a cross-national culture. Most scientists instead rally willingly to their nation's call in time of emergency, and put their skills at the service of their country. Occasionally conflict does arise but it is not very common, and it appears to occur usually when the culture's own values are in flux.

Such a sense of cooperation between host cultures and science is a fairly recent development and has not always been the rule—as the history of Galileo and similar belief-shattering pioneers down to the Scopes trial in 1927 indicates. Scientists whose discoveries seriously rupture the belief-patterns of individual societies can find themselves in great danger of physical and/or legal persecution. But the effects of science on the total ideological and physical environment of the world in recent years have been so powerful that today, for many people, the primary authority for what is believed to be true about reality is science. In other words, science has come to dwarf and even dominate many aspects of the cultures of the world which used to compete with it on its own level.

Let us try to clarify this point.

Cultures are composed of beliefs or cognitions of reality—notions of what the world is really like, as well as norms and values. When

Galileo said that the earth moved about the sun, he was in effect questioning the entire medieval construct of reality as derived from the revered philosophers and theologians of the Hellenic-Christian world. If the earth were no longer the center of the universe, then how could Man be believed to be its eternal purpose and Christ his savior?

To us this conclusion may appear to be the result of a rather enormous inferential leap, but to the theologians and philosophers of Galileo's time the connection was immediate, logical and damning. The Middle Ages had just witnessed the most gargantuan effort to date to unite Faith and Reason (specifically the Christian faith and Aristotelian logic and science)—the *Summa Theologica* of St. Thomas Aquinas—and the Renaissance which had supplanted the Middle Ages had elevated Man with his Free Will and Reason to the pinnacle of all creation.[3] It was this logical-deductive structure which Galileo with his new empirical science so severely threatened, and in fact helped to topple, when he muttered under his breath, "*Eppure, si muove*," ("And still, it moves"). The new science, it appeared, required more than simple faith in certain concepts of reality, and logical inferences therefrom—it also required a rigorous effort to base those beliefs on empirical observations and tests. If the earth does indeed revolve around the sun, does it necessarily follow that Man is any the less a creature of God?

Today the scientist would respond: there are two kinds of beliefs—those about reality which can be empirically tested (in principle at least, if not in actuality at present), and those which cannot. Only the first fall within the realm of science; of the second variety, science can say nothing. It is for this reason that science can today exist in a neutral fashion within just about any variety of culture that man is heir to. If one wishes to believe that God or a Divine Providence directs all events on earth and throughout the universe, the scientist can only respond: "That's your privilege. As yet I have no way of empirically testing the existence of Divine Providence, and therefore, I can say nothing about it." Or, as Ludwig Wittgenstein put it, in a slightly different context, "Whereof one cannot speak, thereof one must be silent."

The dogmatic analytic philosopher will go one step further, however, and will say that any statement which cannot be empirically tested—in principle at the very least—is semantically meaningless. Thus a statement positing the existence of God, by

---

3. See for example, Giovanni Pico Della Mirandola, *Oration on the Dignity of Man* (1486).

definition a spiritual (or "ineffable"), not a material, Being, and therefore, whose existence cannot be empirically verified by science—i.e., by some systematic, reliable and reproducible method (exempting all individual, unique, and hence non-reproducible experiences of Saints, and temporary suspensions of the "laws" of nature as in "miracles")—says nothing and is empty of all meaning. To this the cautious scientist is likely to reply: "Maybe. I once thought all material things were solid. I have since discovered them to be mainly space and energy. Perhaps someday someone will discover a way to define 'spiritual reality' so that it will be amenable to laboratory testing. Science is an ongoing process constantly correcting itself. At the present time such speculations are beyond my tools, my means of dealing with them, and hence I must remain, as a scientist, an agnostic in all such matters."

In other words, science relates only to empirical reality, not to the metaphysical or the transcendental or the poetical or the mystical. Only what can be experienced by the senses and/or their technological extensions, or inferred logically or mathematically from what is already scientifically known, falls within the purview of science.

This does not mean that science has nothing to say about what people believe to be true of the world and reality. Quite the contrary. Whenever a culture or a belief-system contains notions about reality which science can and has demonstrated to be false, conflict will most probably arise. Science will either be driven out or repressed, or the culture will eventually change. The former has most frequently occurred in authoritarian (and totalitarian) systems; the latter in liberal (and democratic) ones. In the twentieth century those systems which have been most tolerant of science and technology have changed the most radically in their beliefs, and very often in their norms and values. Racism, for example, seldom endures unquestioned in a society in which the science of genetics has been allowed to thrive and flourish.

The scientific culture is that set of beliefs, norms and values, which exhorts its followers to study the world about them and to be empirical, systematic, impartial, logical, theoretical, skeptical, and truthful in all that they investigate and report. It invokes, therefore, a certain "ethic" of behavior, based upon a certain "philosophy" or worldview of (1) the scientist's view of reality: basically physical (as the physical scientist would define it); (2) his role with regard to reality: impartial investigation; (3) the canons of behavior he should obey in carrying out his role: inclusion of all relevant data and truthful reporting of all findings; and (4) his goal as a scientist: truth and the expansion of knowledge.

This culture and its philosophy did not come into being all at once and full-grown, like Athena from the head of Zeus. It took centuries to develop and for its tenets to be formulated. Any good history of science can detail this development for the curious student. Suffice it to say that, beginning with Copernicus in the sixteenth and Galileo in the seventeenth century, observation and verification came to have a greater call on one's belief than authority, no matter how revered or mighty, and science, as we know it, began to take form. Individuals like Francis Bacon and René Descartes, Johann Kepler and Isaac Newton, Karl Linnaeus and Charles Darwin, contributed alternatively to the development of the empirical and deductive aspects of science. In doing so, they helped to clarify the essential interdependence of factual investigation and theoretical generalization, inductive inference and deductive logic, discovery, verification and validation, which comprise the "scientific method."

Basically this may entail the systematic gathering of hundreds of observations on a particular subject matter, describing their characteristics and ordering them into consistent patterns, constructing theories, hypotheses or laws about the relationships observed, and, finally, deductively subjecting these theories to rigidly controlled empirical tests so as to determine their acceptance or rejection. The order and degree to which these activities take place is not always as precise or as extensive in every instance as the previous description might imply; but on the whole these are the steps which are involved in any scientific enterprise, so that not logic alone, nor empirical observation alone, but the two together, working in harmony, are basically what we mean when we speak of science.

The "scientific method" or logic of methodology is this rationale by which one comes to accept or reject certain theories or hypotheses about reality which, ideally, have been derived inductively from systematic observation. This does not preclude theories derived from imagination, intuition or insight as well. In fact many scientists have testified that the subconscious mind working on a problem during a time when the conscious mind is at rest is one of the most prolific sources of solutions the scientist possesses. Without resource to intuition or insight, many great theories might never have been developed. The essential ingredient in the scientific method, therefore, is the logical-empirical process of verification and validation rather than the means by which the hypotheses themselves are generated.

It is the central principle or belief of the "philosophy" or culture of science that the scientific method is the only valid way to determine the truth about what is commonly called reality. With this belief go all the aforementioned norms and values to which the scientist adheres in his professional life. This cultural concept of philosophy which we have been invoking throughout this discussion is still the traditional one—that of a consistent rationale or worldview, in which certain norms, values and cognitions are all intertwined. It is not that of the "philosophers of science" per se, or the analytic philosophers to which we referred in chapter one. To them only language is the object of study. Norms and values cannot be meshed logically into a consistent overview of empirical reality because value judgments are a different order of statement from scientific ones, and hence must be analyzed separately. If any connection between values and cognitions can be said to exist, it is in the consequences which certain value choices have or may be perceived to have, upon the "real" world—i.e., their actual or presumed effects upon cognitive reality. But more of this later.

The philosophy of social science (whether traditionally or analytically conceived), is simply a subset of the philosophy of science. Its subject matter is different (human behavior, as opposed to animal or vegetable, organic or inorganic, atomic or subatomic), and therefore the techniques of observation and verification in the social sciences may be different; but the logic of justification or validation is the same. Thus if a theory, derived directly or indirectly (intuited) from empirical observations, correctly predicts the future behavior of the subject under study (in other words, passes the test of empirical-deductive validation), one is logically induced to credit the theory with a high degree of validity. If one accepts the tenets of the scientific method—the rationale on which it bases its acceptance or rejection of statements about reality—one is, in the traditional sense, an adherent of the philosophy of science; and if one practices it as well, in the everyday application of its tenets to one's own work and professional life, one is also a participant in the scientific culture.

However, underlying all that we have said about the philosophy and culture of science, is one basic incongruity—and we hope that we have expressed it in such a way that this incongruity has become obvious. The "philosophy" or culture of science, as outlined above, imposes certain norms of behavior upon the scientist, and holds as one of its major directives that scientific research should be value-free—that is, that the scientist in the practice of his profession, in the selection, observation, measurement, description, organization, theorization and testing of his data and theories, should in all things be neutral. His own personal values should be completely removed from the overall scientific endeavor. The incongruity is that this in itself is an expression of a certain value judgment: science is a worthwhile human endeavor and to engage in it one must proceed with strict adherence to the tenets of scientific inquiry—in particular, to the norms of impartiality, neutrality, or objectivity.

Whether or not such objectivity is possible, much less humanly attainable, is a matter which, since the impact of relativity theory on epistemology, is highly debatable. What it usually refers to is the injunction that scientists should not allow their personal values, or their desire to prove a particular theory, to bias their selection of data or their conclusions. It can no longer be held to imply that scientists could, if they wished, remove all biases from the actual act of observation, for bias will always exist in the instruments of observation themselves and in the particular time-space continuum of the observer and the object being observed, if nowhere else. But, personal, ideological, and primary cultural biases should indeed be removed from the scientific situation, if at all possible. Such, at any rate, is what is usually meant when the norm of scientific objectivity is invoked. This will be further discussed in chapter three.

The basic injunction that science should be value-free arises from the split in twentieth century philosophy between the analytic and normative philosophers which we discussed in chapter one. Instead of the fundamental connection being retained between what have been called the cognitive and moral branches of philosophy—what one knows (or believes one knows) about reality and how one should behave, epistemology and ethics, ("Virtue is Knowledge")—a split developed from the failure on the part of philosophers in general to demonstrate to the satisfaction of analytic philosophers in particular (and before them to David Hume) the existence of any logical or necessary relationship between the two. In other words, "what is" could in no way serve as an exclusive basis for determining "what ought to be." Logic cannot be used to derive moral or ethical statements from factual ones. However, the fact that acceptance of the scientific enterprise does imply adherence to a certain code of behavior on the part of the scientist, constitutes, to some minds at any rate, a bit of an anomaly. The analytic philosopher of science is not likely to agree to this, however. To him, acceptance of the scientific method is not so much an unreasoned act of faith as a logical conclusion to a factual, hence true, statement about procedure: To be scientific means to be impartial. By being objective and truthful one obtains knowledge. No other method has been known to accomplish the same thing to the degree that the scientific method has.

The act of faith, however, lies in this very acceptance of science itself as a worthwhile endeavor—the desire to know about reality and to be able to deal with it. The scientist bases his acceptance of science upon what has been called the "common sense" of science[4]—the fact that science and the scientific method succeed where other endeavors fail. Science actually permits one to deal successfully with one's environment by enabling one to predict how it will behave under certain circumstances. It reveals "laws" of "nature" or of physical reality, which allow one to "cope" and to "survive." It works; if it did not, the scientist would not accept it, but would look instead for some other method or rationale which might. This was the reason for the development of empirical science to begin with, and for its tremendous success since the seventeenth century. But to be a scientist means that one does in fact want to know about reality, one does want to be able to deal with one's environment, to predict how it will behave under certain circumstances, so that one can either adjust to it or change it in some way. It means that one does *indeed* wish to survive. To be a scientist, in other words, is to accept this goal, this value, and to work consciously for its realization.

Thus a method-bound value-free science is in actual fact grounded upon the "ethic" of this cultural philosophy of science. Simply to be a scientist is to opt for the scientific culture and all that it implies: to be a scientist means to choose the scientific way of behaving. It means that one expresses a faith in the value of science to begin with, and agreement with the empirical and logical conclusion based upon its continued success: the scientific method is the best way to achieve one's objective—to understand "reality." And since it is an assertion of faith, it also indirectly implies that goals other than "survival" or even knowledge "for its own sake" may be of greater value, and that others may believe there are different ways of conceiving and understanding "reality" (not all of which may be "physical"): through religion, contemplation or

4. See J. Bronowski, *The Common Sense of Science* (Cambridge: Harvard University Press, 1958).

meditation, through communing with nature, through the use of mind-expanding drugs, through experimentation with extrasensory perception, mysticism, or whatever.

It is the consensus of the scientific community on this matter, this faith in the value of science and the scientific method, which enables the observer to distinguish the scientific culture from all others and in fact to demonstrate that it exists. For it shares all or almost all the essential criteria which anthropologists have established for the existence of a culture—a fairly coherent set of beliefs, norms and values, and a society to live by them.

And, as long as this culture, through adherence to its principal philosophical norms and values, continues to attain a fair degree of success in achieving its major goal—demonstrable truth and knowledge of reality—it will continue to flourish and attract additional adherents. But let its view of truth falter, or the physical or social reality it seeks to reveal pale before the "higher ideals" which men also from time to time require to round out their lives, then that scientific culture may also weaken and falter. For men are simply men, and their notions of what is needed to make their lives meaningful are subject to as many variations and changes as are their social and physical environments. And change (or motion), after all, is, as far as we know, an essential ingredient of existence.

Suggested Readings

Apter, David E., ed. *Ideology and Discontent.* New York: The Free Press of Glencoe, 1964.

Barbour, Ian G. *Issues in Science and Religion.* Englewood Cliffs, N. J.: Prentice-Hall, 1966.

Bronowski, Jacob. *The Common Sense of Science.* Cambridge, Mass.: Harvard University Press, 1958.

Carnap, Rudolf. "The Elimination of Metaphysics Through Logical Analysis of Language." In *Logical Positivism,* edited by A. J. Ayer, pp. 60-81. Glencoe, Ill.: The Free Press, 1959.

Connolly, William E. *Political Science and Ideology.* New York: Atherton Press, 1967.

Eddington, Sir Arthur. *The Nature of the Physical World.* Ann Arbor: University of Michigan Press, 1958.

Geertz, Clifford. "Ideology as a Cultural System." In *Ideology and Discontent,* edited by David Apter, pp. 47-76. New York: The Free Press of Glencoe, 1964.

Kaplan, Abraham. *The New World of Philosophy,* chapter one. New York: Vintage Books, 1961.

Kluckhohn, Clyde. *Culture and Behavior.* Edited by Richard Kluckhohn. New York: The Free Press, 1962.

Kroeber, A. L., and Clyde Kluckhohn. *Culture.* New York: Vintage Books, 1963.

Kuhn, Thomas S. *The Structure of Scientific Revolutions.* Chicago: University of Chicago Press, 1962.

Passmore, J. A. "Can the Social Sciences Be Value-Free?" In *Readings in the Philosophy of Science,* edited by Herbert Feigl and May Brodbeck, pp. 674-76. New York: Appleton-Century-Crofts, 1953.

CHAPTER III

Epistemology

Prior to this chapter, a great deal of the terminology of this book may have been somewhat confusing to the beginning student. Several words were left undefined in order not to have the main line of the discussion interrupted by too many detours. Now, however, we shall begin at the beginning. We shall demonstrate how the simplest concepts come into being and shall explain the meaning of some of the more difficult terms used to express that process, and the method by which these concepts grow into systems of ideas which may be tested scientifically. The first phase of the discussion has to do with that somewhat mystifying discipline, epistemology, and its sometimes ominous output, knowledge theory. The second phase has to do with the "scientific method" and all the diverse implications that term embodies. Once again, the student is referred to the glossary at the end of the book for relief from any confusion which may result. Hopefully, after reading this chapter and the next, such consultations will no longer be necessary.

Science, as should have become obvious by now, is an activity which certain persons choose to undertake for the purpose of obtaining, discovering, or verifying knowledge. Epistemology is that branch of philosophy which has specifically to do with knowledge; it attempts to explain what it is, and how we know what we know, if indeed we know anything at all. Theories of knowledge, or schools of epistemology, range all the way from radical skepticism ("we can know nothing at all") to radical rationalism ("all knowledge is in the mind and from reason alone we derive certitude").

One's theory of knowledge, therefore, is the implied basis for all that one feels capable of saying about reality. One may utter statements about one's specialty whether it be science or law, plumbing or photography, cooking or calligraphy, because one has made certain assumptions about the validity of what one has learned over time, the congruence between the real world and what one perceives that world to be. In other words, under ordinary circumstances, we assume our knowledge of the world to be valid; we feel confident that we can pass on our learning to others, and that their experiences will be similar to our own when they follow in our footsteps. This belief has sometimes been called naive realism, but without some form of this assumption or faith, no science or cumulative learning would be possible.

The curious thing about this particular concept of knowledge, however, is that we cannot demonstrate it to be true—that there is, in fact, an actual correspondence between what we think we know and the "real world." For well over two thousand years philosophers and scientists have been arguing over how we know what we know and whether or not (or to what extent) we can say that we know anything at all. One school—empiricism—claims that concepts arise from basic sense perceptions or experiences. It is the continual repetition of these experiences which causes us to label them for the sake of convenience, so that we can then inform others about them in a meaningful fashion—as the mother does when she instructs her child that a glowing pretty red object is "hot, Baby, hot!"

But the rationalist will argue that sense perception is inaccurate and undependable. Concepts of reality are inborn; they originate not in the senses but in the mind and we in fact organize our sense perceptions to conform deductively with what the mind already knows.

The modern logical positivist or analytic philosopher, on the other hand, claims that *all* "knowledge" is deceptive, and that the mind, which is only a receptor and organizer, not the container or repository of truth, is constantly being deceived: red is not "really" red, it is simply the brain's reaction to the optic nerve's reception of a ray of light having a particular wave length. All conceptual knowledge is linguistic, purely verbal, conventional, and constructed by the mind for the sake of convenience. "True" knowledge therefore is nonexistent and we can never actually know the "real" world.

The pragmatist, however, holds that since the mind can only approximate the real world we should accept the situation (since there is little else we can do), admit that although our knowledge is incomplete and inaccurate, probable and not certain, it will serve us just as well in the great majority of instances, and simply go on with the business of living.

Obviously not all of these positions can be true, but there may be a bit of truth in each. Thus while the formation of concepts may arise as the result of perceptions of repetitions of similar experiences ("glowing red objects are usually hot"), it is the mind which abstracts from each recurrence of the experience a general rule (formulates the concept), and it is the peculiar ability of the human brain and physiology to be able to express that concept in words ("hot!"). The fact that heat is motion and that measurements of heat are actually apprehensions of different intensities of movement is not immediately obvious to the perceiving individual, however, so that sense experience does not necessarily give rise to accurate knowledge.

Experiences are usually inchoate, fuzzy and unclear, and must be refined or processed by the brain, arranged in an orderly fashion, classified, and labeled before we can say that we understand them or have knowledge of them. But the brain, while it has this ability, is still only a fallible instrument, and may be mistaken in its classification and its labeling. Thus it may not be accurate in its processing of incoming information because it may have no previous guidelines (no program) to tell it what to do or how to process the data. It may make up the rules as it goes along. Or its internal structure may make it impossible for it to perceive the actual relationships among the data without considerable trial and error or psychological upheaval. In an effort to verify its findings it may then try to communicate them to other minds in similar situations. These other minds may contradict its original interpretations, however, and it may face the dilemma of either agreeing with the others, or, if unable to convince them of the inaccuracy of their interpretation, of being ostracized from their society.

For knowledge to be something more than just raw experience and tentative conjecture, it must be shared, accumulated and ratified in some way. It is highly debatable whether purely individual or personal knowledge, if it cannot be expressed in that cultural-social instrument, language, can validly be considered knowledge at all. If it is so unique that it cannot even be communicated, it can hardly be verified by independent means. Or, if it can be communicated, but not in a way which would allow others to share in it and test it for themselves, then such knowledge is not, by definition, scientific knowledge, and cannot come within the purview of any scientific study.

The thinking mind, and even more so the scientific mind, if it is not to remain in isolation, must clarify its reasons for selecting one type of classification or label over another, and must weigh these against those presented by its colleagues. What usually happens, however, is that long before any such conflict arises, while the mind is still young and relatively "inexperienced," it is instructed on what its experiences should or "really" mean by the society in which it finds itself. Its perceptions are structured, in other words, not only by the nature of the perceiving instrument (the brain that converts a certain wavelength of light into a sensation of color), but also by the interpretations of the society into which it is socialized (that particular sensation is "red, Baby"). The classifications, the very labels themselves, through which we claim to know things are essentially arbitrary—they are what we, the group which happens to be in communication on these items, say they are, and continue to be only so long as it serves our purpose to consider them thus. ("A rose by any other name. . ."). What we call knowledge *is*, therefore, constructed by the mind, but sensate experience is the raw data used in the construction, and the interpretation or refining process involves a system of interactions between the refining and communicating equipment of the perceiving individual (brain and language) and that of the group with which he shares his experience.

The end product, therefore, is only as reliable as its components enable it to be. The patterns into which the data are assembled are in part determined by the structure, capacity, and observational standpoint of the instrument, and in part by the interpretations and/or critical techniques taught it by its social environment. Knowledge, in addition to being a social product, would also appear to the modern "critical realist" to be both empirical and rational, and not exclusively either—although the history of the development of epistemology indicates a kind of oscillation between the two positions.

Among the earliest explanations[1] for this difficulty which men have in knowing about the real world was that proposed by Plato. He held to a kind of "naive idealism": men were like prisoners in a dark cave who saw only reflections of reality on the cave's wall, in the form of shadows cast by the world as it passed by a fire burning in the entrance to the cave. It would take a truly extraordinary man, a philosopher, to be able to think his way to reality under such a handicap, since reality existed not as we know it but in eternal ideal form beyond the everyday existence of the physical world. Chairs, for example were physical manifestations of "chair-ness," the eternal exemplar or ideal chair, which of course was always the same, despite the many different varieties of chair we might in fact build. We might change our interpretations of "chair-ness" but the eternal exemplar remained unchanged in the "truly real," ideal world.

Aristotle and his followers in the medieval world held to a kind of "moderate realism." There was indeed a one-to-one correspondence between the real world and man's perception or intuitions of it, but in Aquinas' viewpoint, knowledge is conditional upon faith and divine authority—these are the ultimate sources of all human knowledge.

The method which most of the ancients used to establish certainty, and which Aristotle erected into a veritable science, was that of deductive logic. General principles (self-evident) were posited like Euclid's axioms, universal, undebatable and given. From these were derived certain specific conclusions which, because of the truth of the general principles, had also to be true. Thus the syllogism: "All men are mortal, Socrates is a man, therefore Socrates is mortal," was a typical exercise in Aristotelian deductive logic. It was this model of the learning process—deriving certain but specific truths from universal ones as revealed by reason or insight (today we would call them "hunches" or "intuitions")—which prevailed throughout the history of epistemology down to the nineteenth century. Empiricism, based on inductive logic, did not come into its own until the late nineteenth and early twentieth centuries. A series of cracks in the foundation of rationalism appeared much earlier, of course, but

---

1. Much of what follows can be found in any epistemology textbook, but for a close approximation of the scientist's point of view see Hans Reichenbach, *The Rise of Scientific Philosophy* (Berkeley: University of California Press, 1951).

before empiricism and induction could come into their own as legitimate bases for knowledge, an entirely new concept of knowledge had to be elaborated. The impetus of science and the interplay of mathematics and experimentation in the process of scientific discovery—deduction and induction, rationalism and empiricism—is what eventually led to the revolution in epistemology and knowledge theory which is still going on today.

Descartes, a mathematician par excellence, opened an entirely new era in epistemology in the seventeenth century when he attempted to construct an axiomatic system of "certain" statements from which all human knowledge could be deduced. He began by asking what it was that an individual could be absolutely certain of. By pushing doubt back to its ultimate limits he concluded that he could actually prove only one certain bit of knowledge—that while he doubted, he thought, and while he thought, he existed: *Cogito ergo sum*, or the existence of the idea of oneself doubting proves the existence of oneself. All knowledge, and therefore reality, exists in the mind. Thus from the existence in his mind of the "clear and distinct" idea of God, Descartes deduced the actual existence of God—a purely rationalistic and deductive procedure, but one which preserved, for the time being, a belief in certain knowledge.

Toward the end of the seventeenth century, Isaac Newton, working with the fruits of the major empirical discoveries of Copernicus, Galileo, Kepler, and others, elaborated his grand clock-like model of the universe based upon the principles of gravitation and cause and effect. So mathematically perfect did this model appear, yet so accurately predictive of empirical reality, that a major impetus to attempt to explain our knowledge of the world in terms of empiricism rather than rationalism resulted.

John Locke posited a concept of the mind as a *tabula rasa* or clean slate with all ideas, even mathematical ones, derived from sensate experience through induction—a principle debated by the Greeks but left to stagnate throughout the period of rationalistic ascendancy until Francis Bacon, the great "experimenter" and empiricist, saw it as the basis for all learning. But David Hume[2] in the following century contradicted the principle of induction by demonstrating that certain knowledge could never result.

Inductive inference, according to Hume, was based upon the principle of enumeration—drawing from repeated instances of a particular class of events the conclusion that the similarity which

2. See discussion of Hume in George H. Sabine's *A History of Political Theory* (New York: Henry Holt and Company, 1950), pp. 598 ff., or any edition of Humes *Inquiry Concerning Human Understanding.*

each instance shared with all the others constituted a kind of "law" or regularity in nature. However, said Hume, induction is defective in that one could never be sure that what one had observed empirically, no matter how many times in the past, would always be true in the future. Induction, unlike deduction, could never result in any kind of logical necessity.

Also, one could never demonstrate that a particular sequence of events was ever anything more than an empirical correlation; the "law" of cause and effect, as posited by Newton, was for the most part illusory, and only probable in its conclusions. The assumption of the existence of such a law was a convention only, not a demonstrable fact. Therefore one might conclude that the rooster Chanticleer's boasts that his crowing each morning served to wake up the sun had about as much validity as most factors called "causal." Thus radical empiricism was shown to lead to extreme skepticism or agnosticism, and threatened the very existence of science itself. One can "know" nothing; all one is left with is the "habit" of inferring from experience certain basically unprovable generalizations.

Immanuel Kant,[3] a sincerely religious man who was also concerned about the preservation of Newtonian physics, was deeply disturbed by this state of affairs, and attempted to restore knowledge to its "rightful" place. He sought to do this by uniting rationalism and empiricism into a new kind of realism, asserting that knowledge depends upon both reason and sense experience. But to do so and still allow for the obvious imperfections which exist in human knowledge, Kant held that there were actually two kinds of knowledge: *a priori*, imposed by reason and independent of all experience, and *a posteriori*, derived through experience. However, instead of holding that *a priori* knowledge is necessarily deductive and analytic, as one might have expected from a traditional follower of the rationalist school, Kant held that *a priori* knowledge could be synthetic as well. In other words, all new knowledge did not necessarily come from the senses only; the mind could construct new knowledge on its own, without resource to and even prior to any consultation of the senses. The "self-evident" truths of Aristotle, the axioms of Euclid, and the mathematical formulations of Newton, including the law of cause and effect, were all synthetic *a priori*. The mind knew them before finding empirical

---

3. See discussion of Kant's philosophy in John H. Hallowell, *Main Currents in Modern Political Thought* (New York: Henry Holt and Company, 1950), pp. 236 ff., or any translation of Kant's *Critique of Pure Reason* and *Critique of Practical Reason.*

realities to conform to them. We are sure there must be a cause for every event before becoming aware of a cause for any particular event. Thus Kant attempted to save certain knowledge and the principle of causation from the skepticism of Hume, but in doing so he denied the basically empirical nature of philosphical, scientific, mathematical or geometrical generalizations.

Kant also attempted to save moral or religious truth from the same skepticism by positing two spheres of reality: *noumena,* or things in themselves, and *phenomena,* or things as they appear to be. The human intellect can only arrive at knowledge of phenomena, because knowledge is the arrangement of empirical reality *(a posteriori)* according to the order or framework established by the mind *(a priori).* Behind the appearances of the objects of reality must be the things in themselves as they exist before being apprehended and arranged by the mind *(noumena),* and as such they must be forever unknowable. The world of *noumena* can only be approached through faith or the moral will—our moral self transcending the phenomenal world, making us conscious of and bringing us into contact with (among other things) God and moral obligation. Thus, while ultimate reality resides in *noumena,* it can never be known either through reason or through the senses; neither rationalism nor empiricism can operate in this sphere. It can only be "known" to the "transcendental" or "moral" self.

In effect, then, Kant preserved certain knowledge, but relegated it to the sphere of phenomena or appearances only. In doing so he actually joined Hume in undermining science, rather than counteracting him; and instead of reasserting the reliability of knowledge as he had originally intended, Kant separated knowledge from reality altogether and helped prepare the way for the extreme idealism of nineteenth century Romanticism and of Georg Hegel—anti-intellectualism and mysticism par excellence.

Hegel[4] began with the assertion that the real is rational and the rational real. God or the Absolute is Thought and Thought is the ultimate reality. Every truth is the result of a dialectical process of synthesis of two contradictory "truths," and only the Absolute Knower (Mind) knows the real truth. Reason is the "Sovereign of the World," the "substance of the universe," the eternal Idea. And it is this Idea which is perpetually realizing itself in the dialectical process of history: thesis, antithesis, synthesis, over and over

---

4. See discussion of Hegel in Hallowell, *Main Currents in Modern Political Thought,* pp. 254 ff., or any translation of Hegel's *Philosophy of Right.*

again. But while only God has Absolute Knowledge it is man's duty to seek Him out.

Hegel's God, however, is not personal, but immanent in the world, and is in fact, its history. If one would know God (the Real, the Ideal), one must know History, or God's will, as He reveals himself in the world—the World Spirit. True freedom therefore is the identification of one's own reason with God's Reason. The State is the ultimate embodiment of Reason in the world, hence "The State is the March of God in the World." Freedom consists in submission to the State, to the moral will of the community. And History is the "final court of appeal," the ultimate judge of right. The dialectic, therefore, is not only the only method by which one can arrive at knowledge, it is reality itself, for thought and being are one.

If all this sounds mystical—it is, and was meant to be. It is ultimately why philosophy became, as Hans Reichenbach put it, "an object of derision"[5] among scientists. For if this were knowledge, scientists would have none of it. To them, knowledge had to have some relation to what they were doing—it had to be a part of the human endeavor, concrete, here and now, precise, unvague, and practical. Logic, the dialectic or whatever, could not dictate or determine truth, it could only help one discover it. Thus several somewhat new schools of philosophy (and epistemology) came into being to try to cope with or circumvent, rather than refute (how does one refute the irrefutable?), the Hegelian system.

Basically three approaches to epistemology arose from the scientists' revolt against Hegel. The first was spearheaded by Charles Sanders Peirce,[6] the earliest of the pragmatists. It was he who formulated the concept of operationalism or the "pragmatic theory of meaning." Briefly put, this theory held that our ideas of things are really our conceptions of their sensible effects. To test the validity of a statement therefore we must test its effects—that is, we must first translate it into hypothetical form: an "if" clause positing the concept to be tested, followed by a human operation or test, and a "then" clause indicating the result of that operation, something experienced or observed by the person performing it. ("If operation O were to be performed on this, then E would be

---

5. *The Rise of Scientific Philosophy* (Berkeley: University of California Press, 1951), p. 73.

6. See Morton White, *The Age of Analysis,* for excerpts and discussions of the works of Peirce, Carnap, Wittgenstein, Russell, Whitehead, James, Dewey, and others whose works bear on this period. (New York: Mentor Books, New American Library, 1955).

experienced.") Thus the concept "heavy" translates as: "If one were to remove all opposing forces from this object, it would fall." Belief is the establishment of a habit which results from the satisfaction of doubt. The only effect which real things have is to cause belief. Since real things are independent of what anybody thinks them to be, true belief is that opinion which will be ultimately agreed upon by all who investigate, and the object of this opinion is what is called reality.

Peirce proposed his theory before Einstein's breakthrough on relativity, hence he was still able to ask, "How is it possible to say that there is any question which might not ultimately be solved?" He believed, in other words, that truth was ultimately knowable if one employed "the scientific method of fixing belief"—i.e., operationalism.

Other pragmatists modified this concept somewhat. James stated that if you wanted to know whether a theory was true or not, try believing it and see if satisfactory results ensue. This was not what Peirce meant by "performing an operation," that is, demonstrating a correspondence between the concept and its physical effects satisfactorily to all those who investigated, since James' notion of satisfaction was individual rather than public. But James' notion did allow a degree of respectability to some varieties of metaphysical and theological statements.

First a physicist and then the logical positivists of the 1920s and 1930s took up the "operationalist criterion of meaning," or the "verifiability theory of truth," and converted it into the central criterion of all scientific validation. In reaction to recent revolutionary discoveries in mathematics and physics,[7] (among them the construction of several varieties of non-Euclidean geometry, Einstein's demonstration of the inability of observation to establish the validity of the concept of simultaneity, and later Heisenberg's experiments in quantum theory resulting in his "principle of uncertainty" or indeterminancy), P. W. Bridgman[8] first put forth the radical assertion that no concept should be considered meaningful unless it could withstand the test of operationalism—that is, an actual physical test of its correspondence with reality. Persons using different tests for the same concept were actually defining different concepts. (Length measured by a yardstick was a totally different concept from length

---

7. See J. Bronowski's *The Common Sense of Science* (Cambridge: Harvard University Press, 1958), for a discussion of these events.

8. P. W. Bridgman, *The Logic of Modern Physics* (New York: Macmillan, 1927).

measured by beams of light because the measuring operation was totally different.) Thus all metaphysical and similar statements which did not refer to actual physical reality were meaningless, and all knowledge, including scientific knowledge, is relative to the types of operations one performs in attempting to confirm or disconfirm its content. Knowledge, therefore, no longer included such items as mystical or poetic or religious or other non-operationalizable concepts. Kant's *noumena* just did not exist.

The logical positivists, Carnap, Wittgenstein and others, and later semanticists like Korzybski and Hayakawa,[9] concentrated on linguistic analysis and the nominalist notion that all knowledge is linguistic knowledge—that is, verbal, and structured by the language and logical syntax one uses to express it. This position developed out of the earlier work of analytic philosophers, Bertrand Russell and Alfred North Whitehead, who had demonstrated the basic similarity between logic and mathematics, and the "emptiness" or "tautologousness" of both.

In other words, concepts are arbitrary labels, symbols, or names one gives to certain types of experiences. They are not "self-evident," or "intuited" or conceived in some way by the mind or "reason," without need of or reference to sensate experiences. There are no "synthetic *a priori.*" All concepts, even mathematical abstractions, are derived ultimately from the data of the senses, and their actual relationship to physical reality. Their "truth" or "meaningfulness" (to the scientist these two terms tend to become synonymous) can only be tested empirically through the operationalist criterion of meaning. Everything else is logical or symbolic manipulation to clarify and bring out the inferences already inherent in the terms being used. Sense experience, therefore, is the only way one can arrive at synthetic or new knowledge; logic is only analytical—it can teach us nothing that was not already implied in its basic premises. Thus, "All men are mortal, Socrates is a man, therefore Socrates is mortal," may make a good logical syllogism, but the conclusion that Socrates is mortal was already implied in the first two premises. Logic, in other words, can teach us nothing new; it is tautologous. All it can do is clarify what is already implied in the original statements. It makes applicable to specific instances (the particular) what was already known in general (the universal).

---

9. See S. I. Hayakawa, "Language and Behavior," in *Introductory Readings in Political Behavior,* ed. S. Sidney Ulmer (Chicago: Rand McNally, 1961), pp. 320 ff.

The same thing is true of mathematics: "$a = b$; $b = c + d/x$; (therefore) $a = c + d/x$." Mathematics is, in fact, an application of logic and the family resemblance has been more than amply demonstrated by the development of symbolic logic or the use of symbols for the simplification and manipulation of logical arguments. Both logic and mathematics are methods for deducing one fact from another, and are only as valid as their premises. Mathematics is especially empty because, being purely symbolic, it has no meaning of its own—not even the consensual meaning which usage gives to words. It takes on meaning only when the symbols are made to stand for particular entities or values. And numbers especially have no objective reality. When one asserts that "$2 + 2 = 4$," one must ask "two what plus two what?" before one can utilize these symbols in any practical enterprise.

Even when one has answered this implied question, the result on the other side of the equation is simply a statement of the obvious, an identity—two hotdogs plus two hotdogs are, inevitably and by definition, four hotdogs. A logical or mathematical conclusion is, therefore, a necessary one—it is always valid, but its meaningfulness (its contextual relationship to physical reality) depends upon empirical verification of its assumptions or premises. Thus while a physicist may put forth an intellectually satisfying mathematical theory of the universe, or a new system of geometry, that theory or predictions deduced from it must be tested operationally before it can be finally accepted. A logical conclusion, therefore, is no more meaningful or truthful than the assumptions on which it is based.

The impact of relativity theory on epistemology went even further. Up to this point, "meaning" referred, in the semantic sense, simply to the way in which a term was actually used in a sentence—its context. But reliance upon the operationalist criterion of meaning implied that the "meaningfulness" of any concept depended upon the validity of its claim to "truth," now newly defined as its correspondence with physical reality as verified by some physical operation. If this criterion is strictly adhered to, however, a curious thing happens to our concept of knowledge when an operation can produce no absolutely certain results. In other words, when two observers, or even the same observer, performing the same experiment several different times and using the same operations, produce slightly divergent results—perhaps because of human error, or slight differences in the instruments or techniques, or even because of atmospheric or environmental differences at the different loci or times of the experiments (elements which can never be absolutely controlled or completely eliminated)—which results do we accept? To be on the safe side a cautious scientist would probably answer "none—for the moment," or, if they are close enough, "maybe all of them are approximately correct—let's try again to see if we can narrow it down to some more likely result." In other words the tendency at the present time is to accept the most probable outcome, but only after conducting a whole series of tests, and without ever claiming that one had discovered or could discover the "only" or "true" result.

Thus knowledge, no longer being the end product of an act of intuition or reason, or even of transcendental will, is now the approximate outcome of an operation or test which verifies the "truth claim" or "meaningfulness" of a concept or theory. Our concept of knowledge, therefore, must itself undergo change when our method of obtaining it changes. What Einstein and Heisenberg both conclusively demonstrated for scientists in general was that knowledge can never be attained absolutely. The observer and the observation are inextricably intertwined; if one can determine the speed of an electron accurately one cannot at the same time know its position, and vice versa. Therefore, all we can hope to do is obtain probable or approximate knowledge. One can measure a thing again and again and take the average of all the results as approximating the truth. It is for this reason that statistics is considered by most scientists today to be the only reliable method of induction.[10]

Thus while one may depend on logic to bring out latent meanings in already known facts, those facts (statements accepted as "true") can only be statistically validated. All first premises, instead of being universal statements of generality, are only probability statements: "All men are mortal" is conditionally true—assuming that no man has failed to die in the past or will fail to die in the future. For all practical purposes we may indeed consider mankind to be mortal—with an exceptionally high degree of probability. But one cannot say with all certainty that the condition will stay the same forever—simply because one can have no "certain" knowledge of the future, just as one can have no "certain" knowledge of the past. Hence the proposition should really be qualified: "As far as we can determine, all men are mortal"; or, "All men are mortal, with a probability of p."

Thus Hume's skepticism about "certain" knowledge has been largely vindicated, but in the process our entire concept of

---

10. Hubert M. Blalock, *Social Statistics* (New York: McGraw-Hill, 1960), p. 5.

knowledge has been radically altered. Not certain knowledge but probable knowledge is all that man can attain. However, by the use of probability theory and statistics one can in many instances measure the "degree of error" with which our observations are contaminated, and can often calculate fairly accurately the limits of our confidence in our probable knowledge. Our epistemological condition may be less than ideal, but at least we can admit of some knowledge rather than none, which was the end result of Hume's approach.[11]

Modern epistemological theory, for the scientist at any rate, is a kind of amalgam of logical positivism, analytic philosophy and pragmatism. We accept as true those statements about reality which can be operationally verified—or, more accurately, we tentatively accept them, because, while expressed or tested in such a manner that it is entirely possible for them to be disproved, they have not as yet been disproved, and they meanwhile continue to maintain the heuristic quality of being able to explain to some degree of satisfaction certain phenomena which are immediately observable.

Knowledge, in other words, is only tentative. We accept one explanation of reality rather than another because it satisfies—for the moment. We establish as many of our truth claims as can be established at the present time, largely through statistical induction, and in the process admit that they may be shot through with errors. We realize that such knowledge is the result of our own attempts to understand the world around us and that it is basically manmade and hence only as valid as we, for the moment, can ratify. But from these tentative explanations we continue to draw logical deductions which we admit are also only tentative, and only as valid as the original generalizations from which they were extracted. And thus we continue with the scientific enterprise: systematically gathering information, intuitively or statistically generalizing from it, and deducing certain conclusions or predictions which we then test as best we can, through the constant repetition of rigidly controlled observations—i.e., statistically—and eventually we revise and replace our concepts and theories as they are discovered to be defective or inadequate.

This is approximately where the philosophy of science stands today on the problem of epistemology—basically with the thesis of

---

11. See discussion of this point in Hans Reichenbach, "Probability Methods in Social Science," in The Policy Sciences, ed. Daniel Lerner and Harold Lasswell (Stanford: Stanford University Press, 1951), pp. 121-28.

probable knowledge—that is, with truth claims that can be verified only to a certain degree of probability. Philosophy, however, was not the only discipline to feel the effects of relativity theory. Sociology, and the social sciences in general, attempted their own solutions to the problem. Ever since Marx and other social philosophers tried to make history into a science of society—also in reaction to Hegel—sociology had been faced with a similar problem vis a vis knowledge; namely, how in his study of social and political interactions was the sociologist to differentiate ideology from truth, fact from opinion. It is a problem the entire communications medium, as well as the government, is faced with today whenever either is accused of "distorting the facts" to suit their own ideological predilections, or of "managing the news."

Basically the question arises whenever a statement is made that one has difficulty believing: "Is that a fact (true), or is that simply the way he views it?" And the deeper one probes the more likely is one to find that it is both—or rather, that there may not be all that much difference between the two. In other words, the answer to Pilate's question ("What is Truth?") may simply be: "Truth is in the eye of the beholder," or as Pirandello put it: *Right You Are, If You Think So (Cosi é, se vi pare).*

However, as Pirandello so eloquently demonstrated, such an attitude could at best be expected to lead to a kind of disorienting confusion, perhaps even a pleasant sort of kaleidoscopic trance; but, as others have feared, it might also result in total mental collapse, or, if social in scope, in anarchy and chaos.

Karl Mannheim in the 1930s set out deliberately to attack the problem of relativism in knowledge and of "ideology and utopia" in politics. He called the result the "sociology of knowledge."

The solution, as he saw it, was not to repeat the errors of the past by attempting to reassert the existence of absolute truth—knowable or unknowable. All that was dead and buried. Instead he tried to hold out the hope of some objectivity of perspective in what was increasingly believed to be a totally subjective enterprise—i.e., knowing. If, as Einstein had demonstrated, no observation could be truly independent of the observer, if both at the time of the observation were forever locked into the same time-space continuum so that no other observer, lacking that same perspective, could possibly duplicate that observation in every detail, then verily, all knowledge *was* relative.

But, said Mannheim, simply because all observers and observations are so inextricably intertwined, does not mean that there is absolutely no possibility of attaining a substantial degree of objectivity in one's pursuit of knowledge. Instead of holding that all knowledge is relative, he preferred to call it "relational"—that is, related to one's social position or environment. Knowledge, in other words, is neither absolute nor individual; it is socially determined. One approaches the conceptual order from a particular perspective, rooted in the folkways of one's parents and one's social class, one's group and one's nation—and even one's world. All truth claims are colored by the interests, the values, the needs, the conscious and unconscious desires of the group (or groups) which attempt to ratify them.

Mannheim's position at first may seem quite similar to that of the logical positivists and the semanticists who stressed the dependence of knowledge on language—a cultural instrument. But in fact he goes much further than they. People speaking the same language and enjoying the same overall cultural traditions can still differ in what they claim to know or believe to be true. The differences are due, says Mannheim, to their different interests, needs (psychological as well as social or economic), and social positions or "classes." The "social determination" of knowledge is a fact which one should not ignore, but which one should examine, scrutinize, investigate, tabulate, document, and in every other way make explicit, so that one can then take it into account when one attempts to speak honestly and with integrity of what one "knows."

Thus, while Mannheim agrees with Marx that ideology is the perspective of the "ruling groups," he also asserts that reform or revolutionary groups have their own special brand of truth as well, which he calls "utopia." Neither tells the "whole truth"—perhaps because neither can. Each side distorts and sees only what it wants to see, and thus "knows" only what it wishes to know.

The way out of the trap, says Mannheim, is to examine the situation as honestly as one can—perhaps by changing one's social position, or geographic location, or simply by admitting the bias, and then, through contact or even conflict with other groups and perspectives, broadening one's viewpoint until it becomes more inclusive and less "particular" than before. As a social enterprise this means the continual integration of different social vantage points, or as Mannheim put it, ". . . the trend towards a higher stage of abstraction is a correlate of the amalgamation of social groups."[12]

---

12. *Ideology and Utopia* (New York: Harvest Books, Harcourt, Brace, and World, 1936), p. 302.

In other words, truth can be known, but only as a function of the inclusiveness of the social group. By comparing and contrasting viewpoints in the process of crossing, enlarging and possibly even erasing group lines, the "truth" will out. The validity of any belief, therefore, is an index of the extensiveness of the social entity which holds it. Presumably, also, universal (not absolute) truth, if such could be discovered, would be a product of universal belief. Thus the basis for determining whether or not one might wish to believe a certain statement could be the degree to which there is assent to it, or, if possible, consensus.

Mannheim's position on this point dovetails nicely with that of Peirce who held: "The opinion which is fated to be ultimately agreed to by all who investigate, is what we mean by the truth, and the object represented in this opinion is the real."[13] This viewpoint is what philosophers of science and of social science today call "intersubjectivity." In other words, when scientists, being a group both in the cultural and the sociological sense, through their own particular method of verifying truth claims (operationalization), reach a level of agreement on any particular issue substantial enough so that it might be considered "consensus," and the statement expressing it a statement of "fact" rather than "opinion"—i.e., an almost universally accepted theory—then "true knowledge" in the scientific sense and only in the scientific sense is believed to have been attained. Darwin's theory of evolution is one such item on which there is practically no dissent today—certainly not among scientists.

Notice the similarity of usage between the terms "fact" and "theory" in the preceding paragraph. The difference between the two, as used by scientists today, is simply a matter of degree—the degree to which the community of scientists believes in the validity of the generalization or concept being expressed. Or as Vernon Van Dyke put it: "A fact is a finding or a statement about reality on which universal agreement is, in principle, achievable";[14] and, "when a hypothesis is regarded as pretty well confirmed it may be called a theory, and when it is regarded as completely confirmed it may be called a fact or a law."[15]

---

13. Reprinted in Morton White's *The Age of Analysis* (New York: Mentor Books, New American Library, 1955), p. 151.

14. *Political Science: A Philosophical Analysis* (Stanford: Stanford University Press, 1960), p. 56.

15. Ibid., p. 92.

Thus consensus, intersubjectivity, or near universal agreement is the criterion by which knowledge, truth claims, or "facts" are measured in present-day scientific epistemology. All else (including facts) is held only tentatively, and measured in probabilities or degrees of confidence wherever possible. This is a far cry from the vision of "Eternal Truth" held by Plato twenty-five hundred years ago. It is a brutal, unsettling, anxiety-producing reality to which the twentieth century A.D. has been awakened. But if man is ever to attain maturity and wisdom, he must shuck off the comforting naivetés of an agrarian age and adapt to the harsh realities of the present. Dogma, ideology or utopia, can no longer justify his flights of madness and of horror when, in pursuit of the "right" way, he tramples down all in his path. If uncertainty and anxiety are the price of tolerance, so be it. The modern world may well count that to be a very reasonable bargain indeed.

Suggested Readings

Akermann, Robert. *Theories of Knowledge: A Critical Introduction.* New York: McGraw-Hill, 1965.

Ayer, A. J. "Editor's Introduction." In *Logical Positivism,* edited by A. J. Ayer, pp. 3-28. Glencoe, Ill.: The Free Press, 1959.

Ayer, A. J. "Verification and Experience." In *Logical Positivism* edited by A. J. Ayer, pp. 228-43. Glencoe, Ill.: The Free Press, 1959.

Ayer, A. J., and Raymond Winch, eds. *British Empirical Philosophers: Locke, Berkeley, Hume, Reid and J. S. Mill.* New York: Simon and Schuster, A Clarion Book, 1968.

Barker, S. F. *The Elements of Logic.* New York: McGraw-Hill, 1965.

Bridgman, P. W. *The Logic of Modern Physics,* chapter one. New York: Macmillan, 1927.

Brodbeck, May. "Meaning and Action." In *Readings in the Philosophy of the Social Sciences,* edited by May Brodbeck, pp. 58-78. New York: Macmillan, 1968.

Canfield, John V., and Franklin H. Donnell, Jr., eds. *Readings in the Theory of Knowledge.* New York: Appleton-Century-Crofts, 1964.

Carnap, Rudolf, "Testability and Meaning." In *Readings in the Philosophy of Science,* edited by Herbert Feigl and May Brodbeck, pp. 47-92. New York: Appleton-Century-Crofts, 1953.

Cassirer, Ernest. *The Problem of Knowledge.* New Haven: Yale University Press, 1950.

Dewey, John. *Logic: The Theory of Inquiry.* New York: Holt, Rinehart and Winston, 1938.

Dewey, John. *The Quest for Certainty: A Study of the Relation of Knowledge and Action.* New York: G. P. Putnam's Sons, Capricorn Books, 1960.

Einstein, Albert. *Relativity, The Special and General Theory: A Popular Exposition.* Translated by Robert W. Lawson. New York: Crown Publishers, 1961.

Gamow, George. *Thirty Years That Shook Physics: The Story of Quantum Theory.* Garden City, N. Y.: Doubleday and Company, Anchor Books, 1966.

Hempel, Carl G. "The Empiricist Criterion of Meaning." In *Logical Positivism,* edited by A. J. Ayer, pp. 108-29. Glencoe, Ill.: The Free Press, 1959.

Hempel, Carl G. *The Philosophy of Natural Science.* Englewood Cliffs, N. J.: Prentice-Hall, 1966.

Hook, Sidney. "Dialectic in Society and History." In *Readings in the Philosophy of Science,* edited by Herbert Feigl and May Brodbeck, pp. 710-13. New York: Appleton-Century-Crofts, 1953.

Kalleberg, Arthur L. "Concept Formation in Normative and Empirical

Studies: Toward Reconciliation in Political Theory." _APSR_ 63 (March 1969): 26-39.

Kemeny, John G. _A Philosopher Looks at Science._ New York: Van Nostrand and Reinhold, 1959.

Kyburg, Henry E., Jr. _Probability and Inductive Logic._ London: Macmillan, 1970.

Landau, Martin. "Comment: An Objectivity." _APSR_ 66 (September 1972): 846-56.

Mannheim, Karl. _Ideology and Utopia: An Introduction to the Sociology of Knowledge._ Translated by Louis Wirth and Edward Shils. New York: Harcourt, Brace, and World, Harvest Books, 1936.

Meehan, Eugene J. _Explanation in Social Science: A System Paradigm._ Homewood, Ill.: Dorsey Press, 1968.

Meehan, Eugene J. _The Foundations of Political Analysis, Empirical and Normative._ Homewood, Ill.: Dorsey Press, 1971.

Meehan, Eugene J. _The Theory and Method of Political Analysis._ Homewood, Ill.: Dorsey Press, 1965.

Myrdal, Gunnar. _Objectivity in Social Research._ New York: Random House, Pantheon, 1969.

Nagel, Ernest. "On the Method of _Verstehen_ as the Sole Method of Philosophy." In _Philosophy of the Social Sciences: A Reader,_ edited by Maurice Natanson, pp. 262-70. New York: Random House, 1963.

Nagel, Ernest. _The Structure of Science._ New York: Harcourt, Brace and World, 1961.

Northrup, F. S. C. _The Logic of the Sciences and the Humanities._ Cleveland, Ohio: World Publishing Company, 1959.

Pap, Arthur. _An Introduction to the Philosophy of Science._ New York: Free Press, 1962.

Polanyi, Michael. _Personal Knowledge._ Chicago: University of Chicago Press, 1958.

Reichenbach, Hans. _The Rise of Scientific Philosophy._ Berkeley and Los Angeles: University of California Press, 1951.

Reichenbach, Hans. "The Verifiability Theory of Meaning." In _Readings in the Philosophy of Science,_ edited by Herbert Feigl and May Brodbeck, pp. 93-102. New York: Appleton-Century-Crofts, 1953.

Rosenblueth, Arturo. _Mind and Brain, A Philosophy of Science._ Cambridge, Mass.: M.I.T. Press, 1970.

Rudner, Richard S. "Comment: On Evolving Standard Views in Philosophy of Science." _APSR_ 66 (September 1972): 827-45.

Schlick, Moritz. "The Foundation of Knowledge." In _Logical Positivism,_ edited by A. J. Ayer, pp. 209-27. Glencoe, Ill.: Free Press, 1959.

Schlick, Moritz. "Positivism and Realism." In _Logical Positivism,_ edited by A. J. Ayer, pp. 82-107. Glencoe, Ill.: Free Press, 1959.

Stark, W. _The Sociology of Knowledge, An Essay in Aid of a Deeper Understanding of the History of Ideas._ London: Routledge and Kegan Paul, 1958.

Weber, Max. "'Objectivity' in Social Science and Social Policy." In *Philosophy of the Social Sciences: A Reader*, edited by Maurice Natanson, pp. 355-418. New York: Random House, 1963.

White, Morton. *The Age of Analysis*. New York: Mentor Books, New American Library, 1955.

CHAPTER IV

The Scientific Method

The term "scientific method" is a rather confusing one. It gives the uninitiated the impression that one "method" or kind of magic key can unlock the secrets of the universe, and that one need only follow that formula faithfully and all knowledge will inevitably and unerringly be revealed. Needless to say, there is no such magic formula. The phrase "scientific method" actually refers to the methodology or logic of inquiry followed by persons involved in scientific research. It differs from epistemology in that epistemology is concerned with (1) whether we can know truth at all and (2) how we can distinguish a valid truth claim from an invalid one. The scientific method is one rationale (or system of rules of thought and procedure) for accomplishing the second task of epistemology: determining when a valid truth claim has been made. As such, it is an application of the general logic of reasoning and a branch of epistemology. Its primary concern is to establish guidelines for testing the validity of the concepts and theories used in scientific discourse—i.e., for finding concrete indicators for the concepts, and ways of operationalizing the theories put forth in the different scientific disciplines, so as to make it possible for these theories to be either verified or "disconfirmed," as the case may be. Actual techniques for doing scientific research may vary from discipline to discipline, and from problem to problem, but the logic or rationale which scientists use to help them decide how to set up their experiments or test their hypotheses remains basically the same no matter what the field.

One of the more detailed attempts to describe this rationale and its different parts is given by Arnold Brecht in his book *Political Theory: The Foundations of Twentieth-Century Political Thought*.[1] According to Brecht, the "scientific operations" or "steps of scientific procedure" include:

1. *Observation* of what can be observed, and tentative acceptance or nonacceptance of the observation as sufficiently exact.

2. *Description* of what has been observed, and tentative acceptance or nonacceptance of the description as correct and adequate.

3. *Measurement* of what can be measured; this being merely a particular type of observation and description, but one sufficiently distinct and important to merit separate listing.

4. *Acceptance* or nonacceptance (tentative) as *facts* or *reality* of the results of observation, description, and measurement.

5. *Inductive generalization* (tentative) of accepted individual facts (No. 4), offered as a "factual hypothesis."

6. *Explanation* (tentative) of accepted individual facts (No. 4), or of inductively reached factual generalizations (No. 5), in terms of relations, especially causal relations, offered as a "theoretical hypothesis."

7. *Logical deductive reasoning* from inductively reached factual generalizations (No. 5), of hypothetical explanations (No. 6), so as to make explicit what is implied in them regarding other possible observations (No. 1), or regarding previously accepted facts (No. 4), factual generalizations (No. 5), and hypothetical explanations (No. 6).

8. *Testing* by further observations (Nos. 1-4) the tentative acceptance of observations, reports, and measurements as properly made (Nos. 1-3), and of their results as facts (No. 4), or tentative expectations as warranted (No. 7).

9. *Correcting* the tentative acceptance of observations, etc., and of their results (Nos. 1-4), of inductive generalizations (No. 5) and hypothetical explanations (No. 6), whenever they are incompatible with other accepted observations, generalizations,

---

1. From Arnold Brecht, *Political Theory: The Foundations of Twentieth-Century Political Thought* (Copyright © 1959 by Princeton University Press), pp. 28-29. Reprinted by permission of Princeton University Press.

or explanations; or correcting the previously accepted contributions.

10. *Predicting* events or conditions to be expected as a consequence of past, present, or future events or conditions, or of any possible constellation of such, in order either:
    (a) to test factual or theoretical hypotheses (Nos. 5 and 6), this being identical with steps 7 and 8; or
    (b) to supply a scientific contribution to the practical process of choosing between several possible alternatives of action.

11. *Nonacceptance* (elimination from acceptable propositions) of all statements not obtained or confirmed in the manner here described, especially of "a-priori" propositions, except when "immanent in Scientific Method" or offered merely as "tentative assumptions" or "working hypotheses."

Vernon Van Dyke[2] sums these up into three overall requirements of verifiability, system and generality; verifiability includes the two subsidiary requirements of empirical testing and reliability (results must be trustworthy); system means "organized into an intelligible pattern or structure with significant relationships made clear"; and generality involves employing concepts and statements that "apply to more and more objects, instances or events in any one class."

Arthur S. Goldberg,[3] however, sees only two operations at the "heart of scientific method": retroduction and verification. Retroduction is the means most often used by scientists in arriving at theories or explanations of certain observed phenomena—intuition or "creative imagination." Verification (or falsifiability) is the process of phrasing a particular explanation into a logically universal statement which can then be subjected to empirical invalidation.

Other authors stress *intersubjectivity* and *public* or communicable knowledge arrived at by tests which are *replicable* or subject to repetition by others with similar results.[4] Thus while there are some similarities in each definition given so far, controversy exists over whether or not inductive inference from

2. *Political Science: A Philosophical Analysis* (Stanford: Stanford University Press, 1960), pp. 191-95.

3. "Political Science as Science," in *Politics and Social Life*, ed. Nelson W. Polsby, Robert A. Dentler, and Paul A. Smith (Boston: Houghton Mifflin Company, 1963), pp. 26-36.

4. See for example Herbert Feigl, "The Scientific Outlook: Naturalism and Humanism," *Readings in the Philosophy of Science*, ed. Herbert Feigl and May Brodbeck (New York: Appleton-Century-Crofts, 1953), pp. 8-18.

empirical observations is a necessary condition for scientific inquiry. There also appears to be some question as to whether one "verifies" or "falsifies" a truth claim.

Technically speaking, considering the present state of inductive logic, establishing hard criteria for distinguishing inductive inference from retroduction would be difficult. Aristotle was the first to do so, and Peirce revived the issue when he defined three general types of reasoning in this fashion: "Deduction proves that something *must* be; Induction shows that something *actually* is operative; Abduction (retroduction) merely suggests that something *may* be."[5] One of the difficulties with this definition is that induction when properly carried out is actually an exercise in a particular type of deduction, and refers only to the specific observations already undertaken. It is not really inference in the strictest sense of the word.

To explain:[6] After observing thirty-four presidents of the United States one might wish to generalize (inductively) that "All Presidents of the United States are Protestants." But this proposition actually means that "Washington, Adams, Jefferson, . . . and Truman were Protestants; all the Presidents of the United States are Washington, Adams, Jefferson, . . . and Truman; (therefore) all the Presidents of the United States from Washington to Truman have been Protestants." This is, in its purest form, a perfectly acceptable syllogism and therefore is deductive in nature. But to perform the type of operation that is normally meant when inductive inference is referred to, that is, to conclude as a universal generalization or to make a prediction that "All Presidents of the United States are (or will be) Protestants," is to make a statement which has no demonstrable validity, but is rather an intuitive guess or "leap" to a conclusion which cannot be justified from the observations already performed.

Inference (or prediction) is just not possible through induction. As Hume observed two centuries ago, induction can only produce a summary or enumeration of past observations and a "guess" about the future. This guess about the future is what Peirce called abduction or retroduction, and what Hans Reichenbach called "posits" when founded on probability theory. What is usually

---

5. Quoted by Norwood Russell Hanson, *Patterns of Discovery* (Cambridge: Cambridge University Press, 1965), p. 85.
6. The following is an adaptation of the discussion of this point found in Morris R. Cohen and Ernest Nagel, *An Introduction to Logic and Scientific Method* (New York: Harcourt, Brace & World, 1934), pp. 273-79.

meant by inductive *inference* is, strictly speaking, retroduction, or guesswork. When based on probability theory, it becomes a bet or wager: "All Presidents of the United States will be Protestants (with a probability of p); or, when used to predict to a single case, "the odds are (probability of p) that the next President of the United States will be a Protestant."[7]

Peirce's explanation of retroduction or how "abductory induction" takes place, is as follows:

> The surprising fact, C, is observed;
> But if A were true, C would be a matter of course,
> Hence there is reason to suspect that A is true.[8]

In other words, C should be able to be deductively inferred from A, and A inductively tested by C: if C does not occur, A is false (an example of "eliminative induction"); if A is true, C must occur (a logical necessity). As Norwood R. Hanson expressed it:

> Theories put phenomena into systems. They are built up "in reverse"—retroductively. A theory is a cluster of conclusions in search of a premiss [sic].[9]

The beginning student may recognize this process from his course in introductory statistics. There it is usually called "affirming the consequent."[10] What it means is that a person proposes a certain hypothesis (A: All Presidents of the United States must be Protestant) to explain a "surprising" event (C: All Presidents of the United States have been Protestant). He "guesses" that that is why the event occurred. If his guess is correct, C follows deductively from A. But a single non-occurrence of C invalidates (eliminates) his original hypothesis, A.

The risk inherent in "affirming the consequent" is known in statistics as that of making a "Type II" or "Beta" error: accepting A because C does occur, when A may in fact be a false explanation of C. In other words, some other explanation might be the correct explanation of C, or, if the character of the link between A and C is hypothesized as being "causal," a totally unknown factor or set of

---

7. Hans Reichenbach, "Probability Methods in Social Science," pp. 124-27.

8. "Readings from Peirce," in *Theories of Knowledge: A Critical Introduction*, ed. Robert Ackermann (New York: McGraw-Hill, 1965), p. 280.

9. *Patterns of Discovery* (London: Cambridge University Press, 1958), p. 90.

10. See Hubert M. Blalock, Jr., *Social Statistics* (New York: McGraw-Hill, 1960), pp. 92-93.

factors might actually be causing both A and C. Thus C may occur a great many times—with or without the intervention or occurrence of A—because X, the unknown factor(s) is actually the cause of both A and C. To hypothesize, therefore, that A is the explanation for C is to put oneself in jeopardy of coming to a false conclusion.

In statistics, however, one might wish to convert one's hypothesis from a universal statement (All Presidents must be. . .) to a probabilistic one (Most Presidents have had to be, or will be . . .). One then proceeds by taking a whole series of observations and recording the number of times the event C does occur ("enumerative induction") according to the hypothesis from which it is being predicted (or postdicted, as the case may be). One then compares the number of times event C does occur with the number of times it does not, and through the application of probability theory concludes either that C is actually a chance occurrence, or that one can tentatively and within certain limits accept A as a reasonable explanation of C.

Here the statistical risk is that one may set one's criterion for rejecting a false hypothesis too high and that one may actually reject a fairly reasonable explanation. For example, it is perfectly possible that seven times out of ten one might throw "snake-eyes" with unloaded dice; if one did not continue one's observations (continue throwing) beyond the first ten tries one might reject the dice as loaded. But one would risk rejecting a fair set of dice (a true hypothesis). This is known as a "Type I" or "Alpha" error.

Thus whenever an individual is faced with the problem of having to verify an hypothesis or explanation, he has two alternative courses of action open to him: he may either set up his hypothesis as a universal statement from which C must be deduced so that a single non-occurrence of C invalidates (disconfirms, falsifies, etc.) A; or he may convert his proposition to a probabilistic statement and proceed to establish its credibility in terms of a ratio—that is, the total number of times C does occur over the total number of observations. The end result is a mathematical conclusion of the probability that A is or is not a valid explanation of C. Whether or not one accepts A as valid depends upon whether or not one considers that ratio to be a sufficiently high enough criterion for acceptance or rejection. The decision is an arbitrary one, and does not follow "necessarily" from this type of test, as it must when the hypothesis is a universal statement.

Nevertheless, no inference from empirical observation, whether inductive or abductive, enumerative or eliminative, can be held to be any more than a statement of probabilities. Generalizations, even those which serve as universal propositions from which certain conclusions are deduced, can no longer be considered "genuine" universals in the traditional sense (invariant truths), but are mere guesses which may or may not be supported by empirical observation and statistical inference. For this reason philosophers of science today are speaking less of induction and deduction when describing the scientific method, and more of "the context of discovery," "the context of validation" and "the logic of justification."

The logic of justification[11] is a term frequently used as a synonym for scientific method when one wishes to avoid the latter's ambiguity. It means simply the rationale on which science bases its acceptance or rejection of hypotheses, theories, generalizations or explanations of certain observed phenomena.

The context of discovery refers to the way in which one may have arrived at a particular hypothesis or explanation. Traditionally this was considered to be an inductive process, but since there is no one way to do so—none that can be demonstrated to be valid in every instance, as might be expected of an inductive logic,[12] if such a thing existed or could ever be constructed—one simply asks how one arrived at this particular hypothesis. Which empirical observations, insights or "guesses" led one to put forth this particular explanation at this particular time and place? What *reasons*, statistical or intuitive or whatever, might one have for presenting this particular explanation?

The context of validation, on the other hand, is the total process involved in examining an hypothesis once it has been formulated, and raising questions about its validity. Deduction is the usual technique relied upon for validation, but a "proof" of an hypothesis in the sense of a logical or mathematical "proof," no matter how rigidly deductive the attempt, is just no longer possible. Since the first premises of logical syllogisms can no longer be considered

---

11. What follows is an adaptation of a discussion of these terms in Richard S. Rudner, *Philosophy of Social Science* (Englewood Cliffs, N. J.: Prentice-Hall, 1966), pp. 4-7.

12. For one very famous but unsuccessful attempt at constructing a logic of induction to parallel that of deduction, see discussion of John Stuart Mill's "Canons of Induction" in S. F. Barker, *The Elements of Logic* (New York: McGraw-Hill, 1965), pp. 212-38. For an earlier critique, see Morris Raphael Cohen, *A Preface to Logic* (New York: Meridian Books, 1956), pp. 31-35. The original is in John Stuart Mill, *Philosophy of Scientific Method* (New York: Hafner, 1950), pp. 211-33.

absolutes, their conclusions can no longer be considered "proofs" (Euclid to the contrary notwithstanding). It might be possible to "disprove" a particular hypothesis—that is, to show that the predicted effects do not occur—but not without risking a certain amount of error (the predicted effects may occur sometimes). When dealing with a contingent universe, where probabilities rather than certainties are all that are demonstrable, error is an ever-present problem. Today one validates a hypothesis simply by showing that there is sufficient evidence for tentatively maintaining it. It rather successfully predicts certain outcomes and its failures have not been significant enough in numbers to cause us to disbelieve it or to look for another. For the moment the explanation satisfies. We believe we have sufficient reason to continue to retain our faith in its validity at least until some other explanation comes along that may serve us better, either by explaining a greater range of similar phenomena, or by doing away with a greater number of anomalies and thus reducing the degree of error in our findings. The context of validation, therefore, includes both deductive inference (what is likely to happen if our hypothesis is correct?) and empirical testing (how often, out of a total number of tests, do we observe the predicted outcome and therefore how probable is our hypothesis?).

Thus science has almost imperceptibly moved out of the realm of "Reason" and into the realm of "reasons." Instead of having an ironclad logic by which truth or true explanations can be revealed (deduced), we are left with what some consider a weak substitute in the presentation of reasons, both logical and alogical[13] (empirical or intuitive), for maintaining them. Ultimately the weight or importance of each reason which one may propose for substantiating a particular theory may be classifiable or even measurable in terms of probability theory or other more sophisticated mathematical techniques (factor analysis, multidimensional scaling, etc.). But the old-time concept of certainty arrived at by the exercise of pure reason is long-gone and just not revivable. Verification therefore, is tentative only, validity is probable, and explanation temporary.

The process of empirical verification or testing, however, is greatly aided by adherence to certain criteria which have been developed through the long involved history of scientific research. Briefly, these criteria have been labeled validity, reliability and replicability. Validity here refers not to the theory per se but to the

---

13. Not illogical.

instrument used to measure or test the theory.[14] If the instrument truly measures what it is intended to measure, one aspect of the verification process has been taken care of. Thus if a survey questionnaire intended to measure alienation, for example, is so constructed that only party differences among voters are detected, the instrument is defective and one's theory (in this instance perhaps the factual hypothesis: "the politically alienated are to be found at opposite extremes of the ideological continuum") remains untested. The validity of the testing instrument is crucial to the entire scientific endeavor. The instrument must adequately operationalize the concepts employed in the hypothesis (alienation) and it must do so in such a manner that the results will not be biased or lead automatically to false conclusions. Thus a questionnaire must be guarded against such built-in errors as "response set," "loading," and emotion-laden phrases which might obstruct the gathering of accurate information, plus all the other pitfalls which could beset the scientific pollster. If not, all the money, time, etc., that may have been put into the research project is lost and the entire enterprise becomes a futile one. The validity of the testing instrument, therefore, is the primary criterion by which the verification process or scientific test is judged.

Reliability overlaps with validity, and refers to the procedures and techniques used to insure the objectivity of the experiment or series of observations involved in the construction and application of the testing instrument. If interviewers are not sufficiently trained to be neutral in their conduct of each interview, for example, and to record verbatim and without interpretation each answer exactly as given, different meanings and codes may be assigned to similar responses, thereby rendering the study virtually useless. Reliability thus depends on the proper training of the scientist conceiving the project, as well as the observers recording the data, the coders classifying it, the computer programmers and keypunch operators processing it, and the scientist, once again, who analyzes and interprets it. All must proceed so that their own biases (or lack of skills) do not jeopardize the objectivity of the results.

Replicability follows directly from the criterion of reliability and is, in fact, reliability's ultimate test. Thus if all the procedures from initial construction of the instrument to final analysis of the data

14. An excellent discussion of the different conditions of validity, which the American Psychological Association Committee on Psychological Tests has distinguished for determining the acceptability of different testing instruments, may be found in Ole R. Holsti, *Content Analysis for the Social Sciences and the Humanities* (Reading, Mass.: Addison-Wesley, 1969), pp. 142-49.

have been carried out with sufficient skill, competence, and objectivity, anyone else using the same procedures and care should be able to substantially reproduce or approximate the original findings, and in this manner help to verify them.

Verification, therefore, is a function of (1) skill in the construction of the measuring instrument, (2) objectivity in the performance of research and analysis, (3) public communication of all results, and (4) replicability of those findings by other scientists similarly engaged. In short, verification is arrived at by intersubjectivity and consensus.

The scientific method, when viewed from the point of view of functionalism—that is, what does it do, or what are the tasks or purposes of science—produces three general outcomes: description, explanation and prediction. Another outcome depends upon the disposition of the scientists so engaged: control.

Description is generally considered to be the first public action which a scientist undertakes in any scientific enterprise. He records as carefully and as thoroughly as he can his observations of any particular phenomenon or class of phenomena, whether those observations were controlled or planned by himself, or occurred naturally (rolling a ball down an inclined plane or watching one roll down a hill).

Explanation is any answer to the question "Why?" that the scientist can devise which might plausibly account for the phenomenon observed. It is, in fact, the ultimate goal of all science—to construct theories which explain why things happen the way they do. It depends first on accurate description—how things actually happen (what Brecht called "factual hypothesis" or inductive generalization), and second, on adequate evidence (verification). But the search for theory itself ("theoretical hypothesis") is the major impetus behind all scientific inquiry. Without it there is no science. One may collect data and record observations interminably, but if there is no theory or framework pulling the data together and making sense of the observations—that is, organizing them into some pattern of interrelationships, causal or otherwise—one labors in vain.

Prediction serves two purposes. First, by drawing inferences from his theoretical hypothesis it helps the scientist to concentrate on one or two probable outcomes which might either substantiate or "disconfirm" his theory, thus enabling him to test its validity in a controlled manner, either through experimentation or by providing criteria of relevancy for collecting and organizing the necessary test data. Thus certain planets, sub-atomic particles, and all sorts of undreamed of objects of scientific speculation came to be discovered only long after some theory predicted their existence as a method of accounting for specific observed anomalies. Pluto and Uranus as well as mesons, positrons and the existence of hundreds of other objects of scientific curiosity, were first postulated and then searched for when scientists had no other way to explain previous observations or deviations from previously held theories. Once these objects were discovered the new theories were, temporarily at least, believed to be comfirmed. Prediction, therefore, provides a means of testing one's theories.

Second, prediction also provides a guide to action. If one believes a theory to be correct, one may behave differently than if one disbelieves it. Most rational behavior is usually guided by some view of the consequences of one's actions and therefore by a theory explaining why some things happen while others do not. When a scientist predicts certain outcomes, he generally has some fairly well-documented observations to support his predictions before venturing into the wilds of public forecasting. His predictions are likely to be extremely narrow and based solely on what he can demonstrate to be true (probably), rather than broad or grandiose in scope.

Scientists, therefore, rarely engage in sweeping predictions or clairvoyancy, and rarely do they ever fail to preface their predictions by the very wise disclaimer: "If trends continue in the future as they have in the past, and if all other factors remain the same . . . ." For the scientist knows that his hypotheses are usually valid only in very controlled situations, and when all other possibly disturbing factors have been eliminated. ("A chain reaction will occur in an atomic pile *only* after critical mass has been attained and *only* after cadmium bars sufficient to disrupt the flow of neutrons have been removed, . . . etc."). This is known as the *ceteris paribus* (other things being equal) condition under which all scientific predictions are made. Without it, such predictions would be extremely hazardous.

Description, explanation and prediction may not be enough to satisfy the scientist's very human desire for self-fulfillment. Prediction implies the possibility of control, and if a doctor can predict that a certain vaccine will stop the spread of polio, he would be a most detached doctor indeed if he did not do everything in his power to effect control of that disease, certainly within his own area of practice.

Other scientists are not too much different from family doctors in their desire to control the evils that they see in their own line of work. Psychologists, for example, wish they could control certain types of disruptive behavior in societies as well as in individuals; economists are constantly being plagued with demands that they provide some solution for inflation, unemployment, poverty, etc.; and conflict theorists are continually looking for ways to control the more dangerous varieties of their own specialty which they see in labor relations, race relations and international affairs. Control, but not necessarily elimination, is one of the implied goals in most scientific endeavors.

Whether or not science per se aims at control is a matter for philosophers to debate. Most practioners of "pure" science claim they have no goal but inquiry—knowledge for knowledge's sake; those engaged in "applied" science frequently feel that such sentiments only lead to ivory-towered isolation, and that the question should really be, "*Knowledge For What?*"[15] Knowledge, in other words, should have a socially useful purpose.

Purists usually reply that knowledge may indeed have a socially useful purpose, but that this purpose just may not be realizable at the moment. Basic research is essential whether or not one can immediately justify it in terms of social policy or commercial enterprise. One cannot simply gear research to immediate needs or to immediately realizable gains. Great advances, technological or sociological, might never take place in the absence of free inquiry. Scientists must be free to pursue science, and not some sociological goal. And so the argument continues.

In political science opposition to this point of view has given rise to the policy science approach—to the desire to engage in research with a view toward solving particular social or political problems which exist in present-day society. "Getting involved" and "relevancy" are the key motifs of this particular viewpoint. Which role the individual political scientist should choose for himself—pure research, or applied, knowledge for knowledge's sake, or for the sake of controlling social evils—is a matter for his own determination. There are merits to both arguments and so far neither view has been able to dominate the other. Nor should it. A question so close to the matter of individual ethics and personal choice should hardly be made a dogma for universal adherence.

---

15. Title of a book by Robert S. Lynd (New York: Grove Press, 1964, first published by Princeton University Press, 1939).

The ultimate goal of science,[16] that purpose without which there would be no science, is the production of theory—answers to the question "Why?" In everyday language an answer usually begins with the word "Because . . . ." The question "Why?" implies a causal explanation. But as modern epistemologists, philosophers of science, "operationalists," and even physicists have almost worn themselves out trying to tell us, causation can never be clearly demonstrated.

Aristotle, and all his disciples down through the ages, expounded on the existence of four different varieties of causes: material (what a thing is made of); formal (its external form); final (its purpose); and efficient (what produced it). Of these the most important was considered to be the final cause, the end toward which all creation ultimately aimed, the fulfillment of the purpose of a Rational God—Aristotle's Unmoved Mover. Medieval theologians equated this ultimate teleological purpose with the Supreme Good, the Creator; but with Galileo began the tendency to view the world not as ruled by final causes but as initiated by efficient causes, with God as the first in a long series or chain—the First Cause.

This kind of explanatory process fitted in very nicely with the Newtonian concept of the universe as an evenly balanced mechanism similar to a clock or "perpetual motion machine." Once set in motion it could presumably go on forever.[17] But the work of Einstein, Heisenberg, Gibbs, Bridgman, and others not only replaced the entire Newtonian construct with that of a contingent universe, but also substantiated Hume's thesis that cause was a habit of the mind only, and that all that could be empirically demonstrated was "constant conjunction": event X always followed event Y, and nothing more. That Y might "produce" or "cause" X could never be clearly shown to be anything more than a "pious opinion" or "metaphysical assumption."[18]

To the scientist, ours is a probabilistic, not a deterministic world, and neither single-cause ("The devil made me buy that dress") nor final-cause ("Destiny led him inexorably on . . .") explanations suffice in modern science. We look instead to a plurality of

---

16. Perhaps it would be wiser to speak of the "practical" goal rather than the ultimate, since we are speaking here of science in instrumental or functional terms, rather than in its philosophical or normative aspects. The "theory" being discussed in the following paragraphs is empirical, therefore, not normative.

17. See Ian G. Barbour, Issues in Science and Religion (Englewood Cliffs, N. J.: Prentice-Hall, 1966), Chapter 2, on this point.

18. Hubert M. Blalock, Jr., Causal Inferences in Nonexperimental Research (Chapel Hill: University of North Carolina Press, 1961), p. 15.

influences, many factors, each contributing to the process by which events are shaped, with their individual importance measurable in each instance only in terms of probabilities, correlations, variances, regressions, slopes, linear equations, factor loadings, path analysis, and similar techniques of what statisticians call multivariate analysis.[19] The only criteria we recognize for arbitrarily designating an "influencing" variable or "cause" are (1) asymmetry: the direction of influence is one-way ($Y \rightarrow X$), (2) time sequence: event Y must precede event X, and (3) spatio-temporal contiguity: it must be shown that the events X and Y occurred close upon one another ("touching" each other) in time and space.[20]

Even so, the notion of cause is a theoretical one only; the operational or empirical criteria mentioned in the preceding paragraph still cannot demonstrate conclusively that variable Y is a "producer" or "cause" of variable X. The most that can be said is that we intuitively conclude that one influences the other, but cannot empirically verify our conclusion by any operational technique.

Thus we are left with a situation similar to Kant's, except that today we express our dilemma in semantic terms rather than epistemological ones. Instead of saying that there are two types of knowledge, noumenal and phenomenal, we say that there are two types of language, theoretical and operational, and the connection between the two is consensual only.[21] We assume, in other words, that theoretical and operational definitions of concepts and the relations between them are equivalent when the scientists investigating the problem agree that they are.

To explain: A psychologist wishes to test the hypothesis "Frustration produces aggression" ($Y \rightarrow X$). He first defines the concepts "frustration" and "aggression" in theoretical terms. To test his hypothesis he must then discover operational equivalents of his theoretical concepts. For example, "babies who are prevented from sucking their thumbs will become enraged and will strike out at those persons who interfere with their oral gratification." Then, not only must the psychologist measure the frequency with which babies who are denied the privilege of thumb-sucking strike those

19. Daniel Lerner, "On Cause and Effect," in *Cause and Effect,* ed. Daniel Lerner (New York: Free Press, 1965), pp. 1-10.

20. See Robert Dahl, "Cause and Effect in the Study of Politics," ibid., pp. 95-96, and Ernest Nagel, "Types of Causal Explanations in Science," ibid., pp. 11-32.

21. See discussion on this point in Blalock, *Causal Inferences in Nonexperimental Research,* Chapter 1.

who do the denying (an empirical finding), but he must also argue convincingly that the operation he is performing (preventing babies from sucking their thumbs and counting the number of instances they strike back) is an adequate test or measurement of the theory that "frustration produces aggression." *Does* prevention of thumb-sucking result in frustration, for example, and *is* striking back an adequate indicator of aggression? Is it the only response possible? Should he ignore other types of responses as not being aggressive? What if the child reacts with some type of self-punishment—perhaps by holding its breath in rage? This is only a sample of the possible questions. The discrepancy between the original concept and its operational equivalent is often enormous and frequently insurmountable.

Causation, therefore, is not only not demonstrable because of general epistemological difficulties with the concept itself, but also because of practical operational ones. There is no way that we can demonstrate that the operations we perform to test a theoretical hypothesis in any way necessarily correspond to the concepts utilized in that hypothesis. We are not talking about the genesis of concepts (how did the concept "frustration" come into being), but rather of how one concretizes or operationalizes a mental construct, a product of the mind ("frustration"), in order to test it. Does frustration per se exist, or are we dealing merely with a shorthand term used to describe a multitude of different kinds of behavior, all of which *may* share a certain characteristic, but which we *define* to be common, by reason of our prestructured and perhaps biased collective perception? It is this arbitrary factor, this decreeing of meanings, which gives all science and knowledge its semantic and consensual character, and which makes operationalization so complex. For if frustration embraces a variety of behaviors how can we say that one type only best illustrates our meaning or acts as the most precise indicator of our concept?

The scientist who does attempt to operationalize these concepts and who uses them to construct general explanations of the world around him is caught in the empirical-operational trap of not being able to show any necessary connection between his theories and his findings. The only solution, as Mannheim indicated (see chapter three), is for him to obtain as great a degree of agreement from his scientific colleagues as he possibly can. He must present the best evidence at his command and the strongest possible arguments that his choice of indicators is, if not the best, then at least adequate, and that his theory or explanation is, if not absolutely correct, then at least plausible. But still and all, his theory remains only a point of view—a belief that his explanation is an adequate one. As such it is open to disconfirmation at any time.

The validity of the scientific method hinges on the validity of the process of operationalization. The testing of any theory depends ultimately on the indicators one chooses to operationalize it with; that is, the theory itself is only as good as the indicators selected to operationalize its component parts. If they are inadequate, the theory cannot be said to have been tested at all.

Thus theory, which is at the heart of all science, is probably the most important concept which scientists have to deal with. Unless the scientist understands what theory is and what its function is, he will never understand his own function and his role in the scientific enterprise.

Theory, as we have already said, is explanation; it attempts to answer the question "Why?" But there are many different varieties of theories. They come in all sizes and shapes, have many different types of components, and possess different degrees or levels of explanatory power. Thus there are empirical theories (those based on evidence from the senses and science) and normative ones (referring to metaphysical evidence or ethical considerations).

There are narrow gauge theories of rather limited scope, broad gauge ones which attempt to connect all or as much as can be encompassed on a particular subject matter into a single theory ("grand"), and those of the "middle range"[22] which stand midway between the other two, explaining somewhat more than a single phenomenon or class of phenomena, and somewhat less than all (of social or political behavior, or the behavior of all living organisms, or even the behavior of all particles animate or inanimate).

The theories of the middle range, many of which actually succeed in linking up quite a number of different concepts and data into general patterns or systems of interactions, comprise most of what is done in the social sciences today. We have yet to develop to the point where a Newton or an Einstein can put forth a social theory of the same magnitude as either of these scientists' explanations of the forces of the universe.

Nor are we likely to for some time to come. The social sciences are still quite young and the subject matter extraordinarily complex. Computers are only now beginning to have the capacity to handle on a single run the enormous numbers of variables and mountains

---

22. Robert K. Merton, *Social Theory and Social Structure*, 2nd ed. (New York: Free Press, 1957), pp. 5-10.

of data endemic to the social sciences, and sophisticated mathematical techniques like simulation have only just begun to be developed and utilized to duplicate or even approximate the complicated social interactions which daily occur among even the smallest of groups. Thus experimentation, which has been the mainstay of the physical and biological sciences for centuries, is only now becoming feasible in a general way in the social sciences. Theories, therefore, which could never be even tentatively tested on any level because of the large numbers of variables or data involved, or because of the sensitivity of the subject matter (how could anyone test a theory on the origin of war?), are now coming within the realm of empirical science. And until these are worked out, improved, elaborated, and corrected, no grand theory of social or political interaction is likely to become anything other than an interesting piece of speculation—stimulating perhaps, but not likely to be very fruitful.

Theories[23] are also classified according to the degree of confirmation they have undergone. Simply postulating a relationship among two or more variables means that one is tentatively putting forth an *hypothesis* that has yet to be tested or that may be in the process of being so. Once the hypothesis has been accepted as confirmed, or not disconfirmed, it may move into the category of a *theory*. If it has been held for an exceptionally long period of time and has undergone considerable testing, it may be referred to as a *law* (a constantly recurring regularity) or a *fact* (as confirmed an observation of relationships as one is ever likely to encounter). A combination of theories, laws and facts which fit together into a logical pattern and which serve as the basis for an approach to, or view of, a particular discipline or branch of scholarly endeavor, is called a *paradigm*.

Components of theories are *concepts* or *conceptual schemes* (patterns of concepts), which, when linked together with no special attempt being made to operationalize them or test them, may simply be called *generalizations*.[24] Components of theories which have been operationalized are called *variables* or *indicators*—observational elements whose variations can be measured and therefore whose relationships can, in principle at least, be apprehended

---

23. For an elaboration and discussion of each of the following terms in considerably greater detail, see Vernon Van Dyke, *Political Science: A Philosophical Analysis* (Stanford, Calif.: Stanford University Press, 1960), Part II.

24. Blalock suggests that the term hypothesis be reserved for those generalizations which are on the operational level and clearly rejectable. *Social Statistics*, p. 92.

and empirically verified. *Attributes* are those types of indicators which are dichotomous rather than continuous—they are either present or they are not; there is no question of how much or how little of them one can measure. Combinations of variables which may individually be partial indicators of larger concepts and which show a considerable degree of commonality (common variance) may, through factor analysis or other mathematical techniques, be shown to compose what are called *factors*, or operationalized concepts of a high degree of abstraction or generality.

A theory which has the quality of isomorphism—that is, which verbally, mathematically, or physically, simulates or imitates the variables and their relationships which comprise the theory itself, but in different dimensions (larger or smaller) so as to give it a more manageable form—is called a *model*. Its purpose is to make it easier for the scientist to manipulate the variables—that is, to vary the recipe of the mixture, so that the relationships can be tested by experimentation as well as by observation. It is isomorphic in that it has the same shape or form as the original (the relationships between the components remain the same), and therefore it is presumed that it will behave in the same way as the original, reacting as the components of the theory itself would react, under changing circumstances.

Thus if one had a theory about the causes of a particular war (World War I, perhaps), and one postulated the existence of certain proportions of so many variables which had to be present before that war could begin (so much ignorance of one's opponent, so much paranoia, so much poverty and unemployment, so much wealth and under-utilized resources, boundaries of a particular type, so many armed soldiers, conflicting interests of a certain intensity, etc.), and if each of these could be readily operationalized, one might construct a mathematical model of one's theory, feed it into a computer and try experimenting with it to determine if it came close to simulating the real thing. One might then expand one's theory to include, say, world wars of the twentieth century, and construct a model which would then operate at an even higher level of generality. A "grand" theory on the causes of all wars might require tons of data and thousands of alternating variables and therefore computers of a considerably larger capacity than at present exist; but such a theory might, given the necessary data, facilities, resources, and skill, be possible to construct.

Alternatively, one might, in the process of testing and measuring one's variables, be able to eliminate many factors which have only a peripheral effect upon a war-producing situation. One might actually be able to isolate and pinpoint the few absolutely crucial variables, without which no war is possible. Such a discovery would indeed be a breakthrough in the science of politics as well as a boon to mankind.

Such, then, is the kind of prospect which faces the modern social scientist—an enormous amount of detailed experimentation and investigation to be done, much proposing, operationalizing, and testing of theories, much construction of sophisticated techniques for mathematical and statistical manipulation and analysis, the utilization and borrowing of skills, techniques, theories, and even paradigms of other disciplines and related fields, and finally, much communication and dissemination of findings and theories so that the process of validation, replication and consensus making can go forward in the building of a science.

For without this ongoing, never-ending process of observing, theorizing, testing, replicating and communicating, there is no science and no expansion of human knowledge.

Suggested Readings

Apter, David E., and Charles F. Andrain, eds. *Contemporary Analytical Theory.* Englewood-Cliffs, N. J.: Prentice-Hall, 1972.

Barbour, Ian G. *Issues in Science and Religion.* Englewood Cliffs, N. J.: Prentice-Hall, 1966.

Blalock, Hubert M., Jr. *Causal Inferences in Non-Experimental Research.* Chapel Hill: University of North Carolina Press, 1964.

Blalock, Hubert M., Jr. *Social Statistics.* New York: McGraw-Hill, 1960.

Brecht, Arnold. *Political Theory: The Foundations of Twentieth Century Political Thought.* Princeton, N. J.: Princeton University Press, 1959.

Braithwaite, Richard Bevan. *Scientific Explanation.* New York: Harper and Row, 1960.

Brodbeck, May. "Explanation, Prediction and 'Imperfect' Knowledge." In *Readings in the Philosophy of the Social Sciences,* edited by May Brodbeck, pp. 363-98. New York: Macmillan, 1968.

Cohen, Morris Raphael. *A Preface to Logic.* New York: Meridian Books, 1956.

Cohen, Morris Raphael. *Reason and Nature: The Meaning of Scientific Method,* 2d ed. New York: The Free Press of Glencoe, 1964.

Cohen, Morris R., and Ernest Nagel. *An Introduction to Logic and Scientific Method.* New York: Harcourt, Brace and Company, 1934.

Conant, James B. *Science and Common Sense.* New Haven: Yale University Press, 1951.

Dahl, Robert. "Cause and Effect in the Study of Politics." In *Cause and Effect, The Hayden Colloquium on Scientific Method and Concept,* edited by Daniel Lerner, pp. 75-98. New York: Free Press, 1965.

Dahl, Robert A. "Political Theory: Truth and Consequences." In *Readings in Modern Political Analysis,* edited by Robert A. Dahl and Deane E. Neubauer, pp. 56-69. Englewood Cliffs, N. J.: Prentice-Hall, 1968.

Deutsch, Karl W., and Leroy N. Rieselbach. "Empirical Theory." In *Approaches to the Study of Political Science,* edited by Michael Haas and Henry S. Kariel, pp. 74-109. Scranton, Pa.: Chandler, 1970.

Feigl, Herbert. "Notes on Causality." *Readings in the Philosophy of Science,* edited by Herbert Feigl and May Brodbeck, pp. 408-18. New York: Appleton-Century-Crofts, 1953.

Feigl, Herbert. "The Scientific Outlook: Naturalism and Humanism." *Readings in the Philosophy of Science,* edited by Herbert Feigl and May Brodbeck, pp. 8-18. New York: Appleton-Century-Crofts, 1953.

Frohock, Fred M. *The Nature of Political Inquiry*, chapter four. Homewood, Ill.: Dorsey Press, 1967.

Goldberg, Arthur S. "Political Science as Science." *Politics and Social Life*, edited by Nelson W. Polsby, Robert A. Dentler and Paul A. Smith, pp. 26-36. Boston: Houghton Mifflin Company, 1963.

Hanson, Norwood Russell. *Patterns of Discovery.* Cambridge: Cambridge University Press, 1965.

Hempel, Carl G. *Aspects of Scientific Explanation.* New York: Free Press, 1965.

Holsti, Ole R. *Content Analysis for the Social Sciences and the Humanities.* Reading, Mass.: Addison-Wesley, 1969.

Mill, John Stuart. *Philosophy of Scientific Method.* New York: Hafner, 1950.

Nagel, Ernest. "Types of Causal Explanations in Science." *Cause and Effect, The Hayden Colloquium on Scientific Method and Concept,* edited by Daniel Lerner, pp. 11-32. New York: Free Press, 1965.

Poincaré, Henri. "Non-Euclidean Geometries and the Non-Euclidean World." In *Readings in the Philosophy of Science,* edited by Herbert Feigl and May Brodbeck, pp. 171-80. New York: Appleton-Century-Crofts, 1953.

Reichenbach, Hans. "Probability Methods in Social Science." In *The Policy Sciences,* edited by Daniel Lerner and Harold Lasswell, pp. 121-28. Stanford: Stanford University Press, 1951.

Rudner, Richard S. *The Philosophy of Social Science,* chapter one. Englewood Cliffs, N. J.: Prentice-Hall, 1966.

Schutz, Alfred. "Common-Sense and Scientific Interpretation of Human Action." In *Philosophy of the Social Sciences: A Reader,* edited by Maurice Natanson, pp. 302-42. New York: Random House, 1963.

Van Dyke, Vernon. *Political Science: A Philosophical Analysis.* Stanford, Calif.: Stanford University Press, 1960.

CHAPTER V

Mathematics
and Measurement

Science and mathematics have almost always been considered inseparable. From Pythagoras to the present, knowledge was believed to be related somehow—whether mystically or pragmatically—to numbers and their mathematical manipulation. Plato thought God's major activity was "geometrizing."[1] Pythagoras founded a religious cult based on numbers as well as a system of mathematics. The fullness of knowledge, in man's most ideal conceptualization of it and in almost every era, has been heavily dependent upon mathematics.

The actual connection between science and mathematics, as we understand both operations today, is not mysticism or superstition, but a simpler and far more primitive step—one which precedes and is essential to both mathematics and science and has about as little connection with the occult as the modern mind can imagine—we call it "measurement."

Anyone who has ever graduated from the fifth grade believes he knows what measurement means. He has on many occasions personally experienced or actually performed a wide variety of such operations. He has had his weight measured, his height

---

1. For a very brief but interesting account of some of the more important events in the history of mathematics see Hayward R. Alker, Jr., *Mathematics and Politics* (New York: Macmillan, 1965), Chapter 1.

measured, and occasionally his temperature has been measured. He may own a wristwatch to measure time, a ruler to measure lines, and a speedometer on his bike to measure speed and distance. He has probably seen someone measure material for a dress, quantities of ingredients for a cake, and certain quantities of gas and oil for a car. He is so sure he knows what feet, gallons, minutes, degrees, miles per hour, pounds, quarts, tablespoons, etc., mean that he never really stops to ask.

It may be only after watching a science fiction tale on television, or listening to a teacher tell about the length of the Sun King's arms or the width of a Roman soldier's stride, that it may suddenly dawn on him that time is something we measure by the rotation of the earth and is not absolute, and that feet, yards, meters, miles, inches, etc., are purely arbitrary designations, some of which may have had rather comical origins. By the time he gets to high school he may be all too familiar with the differences between the centigrade and Fahrenheit scales and the formula for converting one to the other. And yet, it may still not occur to him to ask what all these "measurements" have in common, why we make them, and what they mean. By this time inches, degrees, pounds, etc., have become so much a part of his daily life that he believes they are actually concrete "things." He has seen "inches" on his ruler, "pounds" on his bathroom scale, and "degrees" on his thermometer, hasn't he? Of course they are real!

But they are only "real" abstractions—analogies, in fact. An hour is one sweep around the circumference of a clock's face by the minute hand; a degree is the distance a tube of mercury rises between two tiny black lines; a pound is one point on a scale away from the zero mark: they are all *operations*. They "stand for" something else. They are "pointer readings" which we take to "mean" or indicate a relationship between two or more objects which is regular enough for it to be labeled, "counted," or given numbers. As S. Stevens put it," measurement is the assignment of numerals to objects or events according to rules."[2] It has also been called "the process of mapping a real object system into . . . (an) abstract (system)" by Clyde Coombs.[3]

Measurement, in other words, is the abstraction of a pattern of relationships from an observed pattern, and the labeling of these

---

2. Quoted by Fred N. Kerlinger, *Foundations of Behavioral Research* (New York: Holt, Rinehart & Winston, 1964), p. 411.

3. Clyde H. Coombs, "Theory and Methods of Social Measurement," in *Research Methods in the Behavioral Sciences*, ed. Leon Festinger and Daniel Katz (New York: Holt, Rinehart & Winston, 1953), p. 485.

relationships with numerals according to some preconceived rule. When we use a centigrade thermometer, we are saying in fact that the temperature of any substance into which we plunge it is analogous to the distance traveled by a tube of mercury which has previously been calibrated according to the temperature of water, ranging from 0° (freezing point) to 100° (boiling point) on the centigrade scale. We have arbitrarily divided up this distance into one hundred equidistant points and we use these points to "measure" the degrees of heat of all other substances to which our instrument can be applied. A barometer measures atmospheric pressure according to the distance traveled by a tube of mercury also—but in terms of actual inches of mercury rather than any secondary standard such as the thermometer uses (water). If we were to attempt to use mercury as the sole standard of temperature—that is, use its boiling point and freezing point instead of water's, the tube would be much too long and our thermometer ungainly.

The purpose of all this abstracting, analogizing, comparing, labeling and, if all goes well, counting, is to make it possible for those enumerated relationships to be manipulated according to the already established rules of mathematics, of which the labels, numerals, are a part. Ultimately, of course, deduction is the goal—the inferring of certain conclusions from specific assumed relationships. For the moment, measurement—the discovery, designation, and labeling of these relationships—must take place before counting, manipulation or deduction can proceed.

As you will notice, the above paragraph uses the term "numerals" instead of numbers, and does not unequivocally include counting within the process of measurement. This is because measurement may take place at several levels, and counting is not a part of all of them. Also, numerals do not become numbers until one has actually reached the level at which quantification begins.

To clarify: two distinct classes of measurement exist, and each has several levels.[4] The first of these classes is called *qualitative measurement* and includes *nominal* scales and *ordinal* scales. The construction of a nominal scale, the first level of measurement, involves simply labeling with numerals certain objects which share some characteristic or are related in some way. One's social

---

4. Coombs specifies six: "Theory and Methods of Social Measurement," pp. 473-84, and James S. Coleman only three: *Introduction to Mathematical Sociology* (New York: Free Press of Glencoe, 1964), p. 57.

security number or a baseball player's numbered uniform are examples of nominal scales. No one would want to perform any mathematical operations on these numbers (or numerals) because they are not, strictly speaking, quantities. They merely identify or "name" the objects to which they are attached. To add the numbers 7 and 43 on the backs of two baseball players' shirts makes as much sense as trying to add their names.

Nominal scales are simply classification schemes and are of the same genre as stereotypes or concepts abstracted from many observations of similar objects. The formation of a nominal scale is thus analogous to the grouping of perceptions into abstract concepts which takes place at the first stage of knowing. The only difference is that a concept may have a verbal name while a nominal scale in the process of measurement utilizes numerals. Thus instead of saying "these are red apples, those are yellow and those others are green," we simply say, "these are type 1, those are type 2, and those others type 3." As Hayward Alker put it, a nominal scale is "any set of categories that is mutually exhaustive (include [sic] all cases) and exclusive (with no case in more than one category)[5]. . . ." No attempt is being made to do anything other than distinguish the different types. We are not saying that type 1 are better than type 2, or arrived sooner, or are in greater or lesser demand. All we are doing is labeling, coding, classifying, the different types of, in this particular case, apples.

If, however, we *were* to assign our numbers according to some preference or hierarchical order, say, "type 1 is in greater demand than type 2," or "type 1 tastes better than type 2," we would then be arranging our objects into an *ordinal scale,* ranking them in some way. A person at a meat counter gets his cut of meat before the other customers if the number he drew from the ticket dispenser is lower than anyone else's, thus indicating he had arrived before them. He is not simply different from the others, he is higher in rank than they—he will be served before them. His number, in other words, indicates that an ordering process has taken place, and not just that of coding or classifying.

Mathematically the difference between the two scales may be summarized thus:[6] A nominal scale is composed of categories in

---

5. Alker, *Mathematics and Politics*, p. 19.

6. See any one of the following sources for greater detail: Alker, *Mathematics and Politics*, Chapter 2; Coombs, "Theory and Methods of Social Measurement"; Abraham Kaplan, *The Conduct of Inquiry* (San Francisco: Chandler, 1964), pp. 189-98, or any good statistics text.

which all those objects within a single category are equal to each other but not to anything else in that characteristic which serves as the basis for the classification. This equivalency is broken down into the mathematical properties of reflexivity ($a = a$, or anything is equal to itself), symmetry (if $a = b$, then $b = a$), and transitivity (if $a = b$ and $b = c$, then $a = c$).

Ordinal scales are arrangements of nominal scale categories into "more or less," "higher or lower" ranks. These categories, therefore, have the mathematical properties of irreflexivity (a is not greater than $[>] a$), asymmetry (if $a > b$, then b is not $> a$) and transitivity (if $a > b$ and $b > c$, then $a > c$), which enable us to place them along a single continuum. In other words an ordinal scale may allow us to say that Jews are more liberal than Protestants who are in turn more liberal than Catholics, and to assign them ranks 1, 2 and 3 along a liberalism-conservatism scale that ranges from 1 to 3.

The numerals in an ordinal scale have more meaning (are more abstract or subsume a greater number of concepts) than those in a nominal scale since they connote rank as well as identity, but they are still not numbers. The intervals between the items ranked, and therefore between the numbers signifying their rank, are not equal, and in most instances, not even determinable. Hence one cannot as yet perform any arithematic or mathematical operation (such as addition, subtraction, multiplication or division) on them. All one can do is compare and order them in "more or less" terms; one cannot say how much more or how much less each category possesses of the characteristic being measured.

Quantitative measurement, the second class into which measurement levels have been divided, is of considerably higher abstraction, similar to the patterning of concepts into generalizations and theories in the process of knowing, except that here real numbers are used to designate the relationships involved, and some of the rules of deductive mathematics begin to apply.

The first level of quantitative measurement is that in which *interval scales* are possible. If in addition to ranking certain objects along a continuum one can also indicate the exact distance between them, that is, determine precisely how much more or how much less of a certain characteristic each category possesses, then one has constructed an interval scale. One can now begin to add and subtract our labeling numbers since they indicate actual standard units of measurement, like degrees, pounds or inches. Thus one can say that a 70° day is 30° warmer than a 40° day, whereas one could not say that Protestants are one point more liberal than Catholics.

One might be able to construct an interval level liberalism-conservatism scale if one could establish uniform units of liberalism by which to measure it. Some political organizations, liberal, conservative, farm, and labor, have consistently done this by assuming that a certain number of key votes in Congress were of equal importance to their cause, counting the number of times each congressman voted "right" on these issues, and giving each one a score denoting the percentage of times he supported their views. Such scales, however, like the thermometer, do not ordinarily have absolute or "real" zero points, but only arbitrary ones—ones assumed or decreed by the persons constructing the scale. One can, therefore, add and subtract pointer readings on an interval scale, but one cannot multiply or divide them. One cannot say that a 40° day is twice as warm as a 20° day because our 0° point does not really indicate the absence of all heat, but only the freezing point of water (or alcohol on the Fahrenheit scale).

If one *could* say that our zero point was a true indicator of the absence of whatever characteristic we were measuring, then we would have advanced to the second or highest level of quantitative measurement, that of the *ratio scale*. At this level, multiplication and division of our pointer numbers now become possible. Not only can we say that Mr. Jones earns $5,000 more than Mr. Smith, but we can also determine that his salary is twice (or whatever ratio it may happen to be) as high, since to earn $0.00 is really to earn no money at all.

Mathematically the difference between interval and ratio scales is that a fixed number added or subtracted from all the pointer readings on an interval scale does not change the value of the interval readings. Thus readings of 3, 6, and 9 tell us just as much about the distances separating specific items on an interval scale as readings of 0, 3, and 6: there are still three units of distance between each item. But if one were to add or subtract a fixed number from a ratio reading, one would seriously alter its meaning. The ratio of 6 to 3 (2) is very different from that of 3 to 0. Conversely, multiplying or dividing a fixed number into the readings on an interval scale would change their meaning but not that of those on a ratio scale.

The ratio scale consists of the "hardest" numbers one can conceive, and all mathematical operations are possible with them. It is this kind of number, this level of measurement, with which we are most familiar. This type almost exclusively has been drummed into our heads all through our young lives by teachers wielding multiplication tables, geometry books, and slide rules.

Unfortunately for the social scientist, however, this "perfect" form of mathematical measurement is not that which he finds himself most in need of in his own discipline. He is rarely able to operationalize the concepts he must deal with on the ratio level. Most of the operational scales or measurement techniques he constructs are either of the ordinal or interval type, and he must, therefore, work with them in a somewhat different fashion.

In the last three decades psychologists and sociologists (and lately political scientists) have expended enormous amounts of energy constructing various types of measurement scales and indexes in order to measure properties like "intelligence," "personal adjustment," "socioeconomic status," "authoritarianism," "conservatism," "alienation," "cohesion," "urbanization," and so on. They have been joined and considerably aided by certain statisticians who have developed the field of non-parametric statistics, or statistics involving "unreal" numbers—nominal and ordinal level tests. But the lack of satisfaction with such results has from time to time been so great that in recent years a trend has emerged in which certain types of ordinal and interval scales have been constructed and treated *as though* they were ratio scales, just so that a more powerful level of mathematics and statistical tests could be applied to the data. Such procedures are not universally recommended, however, and very stringent criteria for doing so are usually invoked. One must know what one is doing and why, before one can justify violating the logic of each distinct level of measurement, and even then the results must be put forth accompanied by a great many qualifying and explanatory statements.

However, the pragmatic argument occasionally wins out. "Let's try it and see what results we get.[7] We are only dealing with abstract models, after all, and we can never demonstrate their absolute one-to-one correspondence with the 'real' world anyway. So why not experiment?" Thus mathematics is admitted to be a purely deductive and content-free exercise; first premises are admitted to be assumed; therefore let the exercise proceed. Most people who do dare to take the plunge carry before their eyes the same caveat as that which faces the computer programmer in similar circumstances: GI/GØ, or "garbage in, garbage out." The

---

7. For an example of one such dilemma and its pragmatic resolution, see Hubert M. Blalock, Jr., *Social Statistics* (New York: McGraw-Hill, 1960), p. 19. See also Warren S. Torgerson, *Theory and Methods of Scaling* (New York: John Wiley & Sons, 1958), pp. 30-31.

computer will perform whatever mathematical manipulation you instruct it to, but if your numbers make no sense, garbage will result.

Knowing that there is so much danger in any such undertaking, one may well wonder why it is that some normally sober and cautious social scientists will still proceed with the experiment. The reason is that numbers, and mathematical symbols in general, are considered by most scientists to be the highest order of knowledge that one can attain;[8] they are the most general, the most abstract, and the most parsimonious: with them one can condense whole paragraphs of obscure language into a few brief symbols. Their precision or exactness of expression, however, is an illusion, for it is a precision which *only* abstractions can attain. The real world is never abstract; it is composed of thousands of *similar* incidents which we, for convenience sake, treat as though they were exactly the *same* when we try to communicate our experience of them to others. Words, concepts, and theories are already at a very high level of generalization, but mathematical symbols are even more so; they are the least likely of our communication devices to be "faithful" to reality (hence "true") because they subsume so many more items of observation within their categories than do lower level generalizations. The higher the level of the abstraction, the less "true" is it likely to be—but, and this is a very important but, the more meaningful for human understanding does it become. In other words, man's knowledge proceeds apace with his ability to abstract; but the higher the level of the abstraction, the more fragile the construct.

Mathematics, therefore, attains "precision" at the cost of "truth." To mathematize means to assume a great deal of uniformity in our data—to force our data into certain exact categories, whether they fit or not. This is and always has been a major problem with the

---

8. The nineteenth century was particularly susceptible to this belief. As Lord Kelvin once remarked: "When you can measure what you are speaking about, and express it in numbers, you know something about it; but when you cannot measure it, when you cannot express it in numbers, your knowledge is of a meager and unsatisfactory kind: it may be the beginning of knowledge, but you have scarcely, in your thoughts, advanced to the stage of science, whatever the matter may be" (quoted by Kaplan, *The Conduct of Inquiry*, p. 172). Kaplan himself later concludes ". . . I would say that whether we can measure something depends, not on that thing, but on how we have conceptualized it, on our knowledge of it, above all in the skill and ingenuity which we can bring to bear on the process of measurement which our inquiry can put to use. . . . To say of something that it is incapable of being measured is like saying of it that it is knowable only up to a point, that our ideas of it must inevitably remain indeterminate. . . . For the purposes of science it suffices if measurability is treated as a methodological presupposition . . ." (ibid., p. 176).

process of operationalization—the translation of concepts into specific operations so that they may be measured—out of necessity one loses much of the data's nuances and subtleties. Also, the process of measurement substitutes one type of generalization for another. In place of a verbal concept (inexact and "wooly" perhaps) one now has a mathematical one. It is for this reason that statistics has become the major tool of the social sciences. For while it permits the use of deduction and therefore assumes a certain kind of uniformity and exactness in the data, it also allows the calculation of the degree to which one's deductions may be in error.

Statistics is a deductive tool for conducting inductive inference. It not only allows us to test the mathematical hypothesis we already have, it also permits us to generate alternative hypotheses by striking down those which fail and forcing our fertile minds to suggest others. It does this in various ways, but primarily through probability theory coupled with the many techniques of significance testing and multivariate analysis which have been developed over the last few decades.

In other words, we take our raw data, arrange them first in one explanatory mathematical pattern resulting from some measurement procedure; we then submit the pattern or hypothesis to statistical testing (as outlined in chapter four), and if our first hypothesis fails to surmount the traps of Type I or Type II error, we collect new data or rearrange our current data into alternative mathematical patterns and retest until we find one that succeeds, one that we can accept with a certain degree of confidence—statistically.

Statistics is not so much a method for induction as it is a deductive technique for testing alternative inductive inferences which have been deductively or mathematically expressed. We hone in on our concepts by the elimination of successive failures (eliminative induction). We do not prove our theses; we disprove them, and accept only those which are less weak than the others. We measure the degree of error in each alternative hypothesis and accept tentatively that with the least error. When we put forth our hypothesis, therefore, it is with the understanding that there is error in it; that it is not as exact as the mathematical terminology of our measurements would lead us to believe; and that the probability of its being accurate is "p" or the result of whatever test we have applied.

Probability theory is the major statistical tool for testing hypotheses because all knowledge or inductive inference is the result of sampling, and probability theory enables us to measure the degree to which our sample approximates the real world.

To explain: Whenever we formulate a concept or hypothesis we do so on the basis of a limited number of observations—whatever happens to be available to us. We usually do so in an unsystematic fashion, and therefore our concepts and their interpretations are generally vague and difficult to clarify. Probability theory enables us to define the universe of observations upon which we intend to base our concepts and hypotheses, and to draw samples from it systematically according to a specific rule. It allows us to state that since our sample is representative of all the items about which we intend to generalize, and since our hypothesis is based on the observation of the behavior of those units in our sample, that hypothesis is believed to be accurate within the limits of confidence which we have in our sample and according to the probability of accuracy predicted by our tests. Our sample mean, in other words, comes close to approximating the actual population mean of all the items we are attempting to study and to generalize about. It tells us how close we may be to reality—the impossible-to-observe totality we speak about when we say "All men are mortal," or "all x are y." Probability theory lays down the rules, therefore, by which we draw those observational samples which constitute the raw data for our construction of hypotheses, and it is also the major tool with which we test the validity of the measurements and other mathematical manipulations performed on the data by which our hypotheses were operationalized.

The application of a statistical test per se, therefore, does not take place until the very last stage of the analytical procedure, after all observations and measurements through scales and indexes have already been carried out. But its rules for testing must be kept in mind at the earliest stages of our research design—when we are drawing the sample upon which our observations and hypotheses are to be based. Statistics is thus the final check on the validity of our hypotheses, how they were operationalized, and their measurements, no matter how complex or pragmatic or aesthetically pleasing the mathematics of those measurements may be. It brings us down to earth again by reminding us of the fallibility of our reasoning processes and of the basically mechanical and empty nature of mathematics and of logic in general, and of the opacity of observation per se. Statistics "doth make cowards of us all" by making us realize the tenuousness of our conclusions, but it also lends a degree of courage to our cowardice by helping us ascertain how close to reality our conclusions may be.

By this time it should be perfectly clear that measurement is the process by which we operationalize our concepts (hypotheses, theories, laws, etc.), and statistics is the technique by which we validate our measurements. The purpose of all this is to provide us with clear, precise knowledge or "science" (*scientia*). It is based on the assumption that "ideal" (not "real") knowledge is mathematical, and that statistics is the needed corrective to indicate the error in the ideal—to make it "real." It may also put us in the somewhat anomalous position of suggesting that quality is "real" and quantity "ideal"—a position from which we shall partially depart in a moment, but which requires some exploration.

To explain: the two classes of measurement we mentioned earlier in this chapter were called qualitative and quantitative. Quality, as most proponents of mathematics and statistics will tell you, is that property which we attribute to vague or difficult-to-operationalize concepts. They may actually be composed of several different concepts, all overlapping and intertwined and therefore difficult if not impossible to extricate from one another. We may give one such phenomenon a name, or rank different species of that phenomenon into higher or lower orders, but that is all. Beauty is an example of a quality. Thus we may have visual beauty, spiritual beauty, aural beauty, facial beauty, beauty of personality, physical beauty, etc.

Let us fantasize for a moment. Suppose we say that Miss America is more beautiful than the first and second runners-up because she has more facial, physical, personal, spiritual, etc., beauty, but we could not tell precisely how much more of each or which one counted more in our estimates. The fact that we did somehow weigh each girl against the others and came to a conclusion about which one was in possession of the "most" beauty substantiates the fact that measurement per se did take place.

Quantitative measurement must be able to go one step further, however. It must be able to say how much more beautiful Miss America is than the others. Hence the use of tape measures to operationalize "physical beauty," questions to probe spiritual beauty, poise, and depth of personality; talent contests for aural beauty or tests of physical aptitude and agility; and, finally, judges to allot "points" for each component of beauty and thus to produce votes—a semblance of hard quantitative data.

We have thus arrived at what may be postulated to be an interval scale of measurement. We know precisely how many points each judge gave Miss "A" and therefore how many more "degrees" of beauty she possesses than all the other contestants. We cannot yet say that she is twice as beautiful or one-third more beautiful than the next runner-up, unless we are willing to admit to the existence of some absolute standard of non-beauty ("0"). If we declare that no votes means no beauty, we may have made an unsupportable statement, for beauty is still basically a matter of tastes—cultural as well as individual.

If we wish to validate our thesis, however—that "female" beauty is composed of the characteristics we selected to measure, and that Miss America has more of these characteristics than any other contestant (Women's Liberation notwithstanding)—we might proceed to do so by survey techniques, random sampling of the convention hall audience, perhaps, and probability theory. But our conclusions will only be as valid as our sample and the assumptions we build into our measuring instrument, and, therefore, "beauty," for all times, places, and persons, will remain basically undefined.

Does this mean that we will never truly "know" beauty? If all we can do is measure one definition of beauty for this time and place and contest, how valid can we say our knowledge of it is? Statistics will tell us the degree of error which exists in our present attempt at measurement (the opinion of the convention hall audience) but can it indicate how close we are to comprehending the ideal?

The operationalist will answer—nonsense! Beauty is what we measure; it is what we say it is, here and now. It is the end product of our measurement process. The ideal, in fact the concept itself, is mental only; it exists only in the mind, and we have created it. If it is an ideal, we alone have made it that.

To a great extent the operationalist is correct. Concepts have semantic meaning only—they vary in content from culture to culture and from day to day. Measurement is a convenience; it is a technique we have devised to bring order into our own thought processes. Its approximation to reality is as tenuous as the concepts themselves. But then, this is what we mean by knowledge: an ordering of our experiences into certain patterns so as to make them intelligible and meaningful to us. Measurement is the numerical labeling of those concepts so as to be able to manipulate them mathematically for the sake of inference—to make them *more* meaningful.

The distinction between quality and quantity is the difference between different levels of operationalization and measurement—of more or less meaning. Instead of being contradictory or opposites, they are simply terms used to indicate the degree to which certain concepts have been successfully measured. They are poles on a continuum, so to speak, that merge into one another somewhere in between. Concepts at the qualitative end of the continuum are vague, more complex, perhaps, but harder to measure, and hence less "meaningful" than those at the quantitative end. Qualities may not be any the less abstract than quantities but we are less certain of their meaning. In some instances they may be closer to the "inchoateness" or "ineffableness" of raw experience than they are to the precision and clarity of knowledge. We have not as yet agreed upon the indicators to be used and the scales or indexes to be devised by which to operationalize and measure them. When we do, the problems of validity, reliability, replicability and all those characteristics which go into the making of scientific consensus and intersubjectivity will then have to be dealt with, meanings will approach clarity as our definitions approach measurability, and the "ideal" of knowledge (science, "organized experience") will be within our grasp—that is, until usage changes the content of the concepts, perhaps, or better indicators and indexes are conceived, or entirely new experiences, concepts or ways of viewing reality are added to the context of our lives.

And so it goes—experience, conceptualization, operationalization, measurement, inference, statistical testing, validation, revision—until the cycle begins again, as with science in general. The problem of knowledge is not something that can be settled once and for all. If it were, we would be gods and knowledge would be no problem. But under whatever label we study the problem—epistemology, scientific method, the measurement of meaning, etc., it is all basically the same. The mystery of how we know anything at all may be so great that, as Abraham Kaplan put it,[9] it might be wiser for us to concentrate on how we can best use the knowledge we already have to learn more of what we do not know. This is what mathematics and statistics were devised to help us to do. And this is precisely what the entire scientific endeavor is all about—theory building as well as operationalization, discovery as well as validation, induction as well as deduction, and finally, intersubjectivity.

---

9. *The Conduct of Inquiry*, p. 233.

Suggested Readings

Alker, Hayward R., Jr. *Mathematics and Politics.* New York: Macmillan, 1965.

Arrow, Kenneth J. "Mathematical Models in the Social Sciences." In *The Policy Sciences,* edited by Daniel Lerner and Harold D. Lasswell, pp. 129-54. Stanford: Stanford University Press, 1951.

Bauer, Raymond A. *Social Indicators.* Cambridge, Mass. M.I.T. Press, 1966.

Blalock, Hubert M., Jr. "The Measurement Problem: A Gap Between the Languages of Theory and Research." *Methodology in Social Research,* edited by Hubert M. Blalock, Jr., and Ann B. Blalock, pp. 5-27. New York: McGraw-Hill, 1968.

Blalock, Hubert M., Jr. *Theory Construction, From Verbal to Mathematical Formulations.* Englewood Cliffs, N. J.: Prentice-Hall, 1969.

Brodbeck, May. "Models, Meaning and Theories." In *Readings in the Philosophy of the Social Sciences,* edited by May Brodbeck, pp. 579-600. New York: Macmillan, 1968.

Buchanan, William. *Understanding Political Variables.* New York: Charles Scribner's Sons, 1969.

Coleman, James S. *Introduction to Mathematical Sociology.* New York: The Free Press of Glencoe, 1964.

Coombs, Clyde H. "Theory and Methods of Social Measurement." In *Research Methods in the Behavioral Sciences,* edited by Leon Festinger and Daniel Katz, pp. 471-535. New York: Holt, Rinehart and Winston, 1953.

Hempel, Carl G. "On the Nature of Mathematical Truth." In *Readings in the Philosophy of Science,* edited by Herbert Feigl and May Brodbeck, pp. 148-62. New York: Appleton-Century-Crofts, 1953.

Kaplan, Abraham. *The Conduct of Inquiry,* chapter five. San Francisco: Chandler, 1964.

Kemeny, John G. "Mathematics Without Numbers." In *Quantity and Quality, The Hayden Colloquium on Scientific Method and Concept,* edited by Daniel Lerner, pp. 35-51. New York: The Free Press of Glencoe, 1961.

Lazarsfeld, Paul F. "Evidence and Inference in Social Research." In *Evidence and Inference, The Hayden Colloquium on Scientific Method and Concept,* edited by Daniel Lerner, pp. 107-38. Glencoe, Ill.: The Free Press, 1959.

Lerner, Daniel. "Introduction: On Quantity and Quality." In *Quantity and Quality, The Hayden Colloquium on Scientific Method and Concept,* edited by Daniel Lerner, pp. 11-34. New York: The Free Press of Glencoe, 1961.

Osgood, Charles E., George J. Suci, and Percy H. Tannenbaum. *The Measurement of Meaning*. Urbana: University of Illinois Press, 1957.

Torgerson, Warren S. *Theory and Methods of Scaling*. New York: John Wiley and Sons, 1958.

CHAPTER VI

Political Science and the Behavioral Revolution

In chapter one we mentioned that political science is today classified as one of the social sciences and that considerable trauma had been connected with the events by which it became one. We said that this development was the result of the "behavioral revolution." We now come to the question of what all this means and how it happened.

Surprising as it may seem, political science is a fairly new academic discipline. It is also basically an American creation. Despite the fact that books and treatises on politics and political philosophy had been written for well over two thousand years, the incorporation of the study of political science into the curricula of colleges and universities did not occur until the latter part of the nineteenth century in this country, and only "with some difficulty"[1]

---

1. Maurice Duverger, *An Introduction to the Social Sciences* (New York: Frederick A. Praeger, 1964), p. 46.

in Europe after 1945. Like almost every other discipline having to do with the study of man (the humanities) it was originally considered a branch of philosophy. Its method therefore was basically deductive, proceeding from certain assumptions, usually ethical or normative, to certain conclusions concerning the realization of those norms in everyday life. Its main goal was the achievement of the ideal political system under which men might live in peace and harmony with each other.

Almost all of the "classic" treatises on political life were of this type, from Plato to Hegel. One outstanding exception was the work of that "devil incarnate," Niccolò Machiavelli. Italy in the sixteenth century was deeply enmeshed in political corruption, and Machiavelli had been too deeply involved in its machinations and convolutions for him to be able to deceive himself about the practicality of any ideal political system. Instead, he used his experiences to help him formulate certain prescriptions of behavior for "the Prince" who wanted to establish or maintain, not "the best," but simply a stable political regime. Inherent in his advice was a particular view of human nature which led him to believe that men would react in certain ways to certain types of situations. He was, therefore, the first empirical (non-normative) political scientist in the modern sense: from his experiences he drew certain conclusions about human behavior, and using these conclusions predicted outcomes for various prescribed courses of action on the part of the Prince. He was thus also the first "policy" scientist. His amorality was frequently condemned as *immorality*, however, so shocking were some of those prescriptions. But he did little more than make explicit some of the principles of statecraft which had long been practiced wherever power was at stake.

The nineteenth century saw the expansion of the Industrial Revolution and with it the growth of what can only be called the "cult" of science. Newton's mechanistic view of the world had come into its own, and "laws" were being sought everywhere for all things, including human history and society. History was being explained in terms of cyclical laws of one sort or another, whether Vico's triads or Hegel's dialectic. Economics, or "political economy," was found subject to the laws of supply and demand, diminishing returns, overpopulation, etc., by Adam Smith, the Physiocrats, Malthus, Ricardo, and others. Montesquieu had already had considerable success with his application of Newton to politics in the "checks and balances" concept which had been enshrined in the American constitution. And finally, social philosophers like Henri de Saint-Simon and Auguste Comte were calling for the development of a political or social science[2] ("social physics" or "sociology" Comte called it) which would discover laws of social and political interaction and development. To Comte, the age of science or positivism was to be the capstone of all human history; science, the religion and philosophy of positivism, and the scientific method applied to all social life, would ultimately result in the perfect society, directed not by a Platonic philosopher-king but by scientific priests or sociologists. It would be their duty to interpret sociological principles to the people through their teaching and preaching, shaping public opinion and acting as consultants to "the secular arm of the law." Thus social scientists were to be both the discoverers of the laws of society, politics and "progress," and the teacher-advisers of societies and governments.[3]

The break between philosophy and social science was begun early in the nineteenth century, but it was imperfectly effected. Marx was the next major thinker to elaborate a science of social, economic and political development (or sociology), converting Hegel's "laws" of history to his own use. However, so heavily "political" were the implications of his theories that not until the twentieth century was much thought given to his "scientific" contributions,[4] and even then, the ideological framework of his system was so pervasive as to make the distinction between science and philosophy meaningless in his writings and in those of many of his followers.

Many European sociologists did try to make a clear break from philosophy, however, as Durkheim, Weber, Pareto, and others proceeded with their empirical investigations and theory building. Mendel and Darwin added the tremendous impetus of biological law to the search for similar "laws" of social evolution, and Herbert Spencer did his best to provide them.[5] Sociology, therefore, was

---

2. Despite the fact that some authors, like Robert von Mohl and Heinrich Ahrens, were calling for two distinct sciences of politics and of society, neither Saint-Simon nor Comte clearly made this distinction; the science of society was to form the foundation of the art of politics, and in fact, sociology was regarded by Comte as "the perfected political science of the future." Rousseau had earlier been among the first to distinguish between a social and a political "contract," but a separation between the two disciplines was not to be formalized until the latter part of the nineteenth century. See Howard Becker and Harry Elmer Barnes, *Social Thought from Lore to Science*, 3rd ed., vol. 2, (New York: Dover Publications, 1961), pp. 549 ff., for discussions of Von Mohl, Saint-Simon, and Comte.

3. Compare with David Easton's analysis of the three roles which political scientists may take in modern society, p. 98 of this book.

4. M. Duverger, *An Introduction to the Social Sciences*, p. 18.

5. For a summary of such "laws" see Becker and Barnes, *Social Thought from Lore to Science*, p. 668.

well on its way to becoming a separate empirical discipline oriented toward science more than philosophy, and dedicated to the search for laws of social behavior and development.

But the fate of political science was not at all so rosy. In Europe, in fact, it would be difficult to try to find the thinker who bothered to distinguish it from sociology. All of those European authors of the nineteenth and early twentieth centuries who are today considered forerunners of modern empirical political science were sociologists first, and are still thought of as such: Max Weber, Vilfredo Pareto, Gaetano Mosca (the lone politican in the group), Robert Michels, Georges Sorel, and many others. If one wanted to study empirical political science in a European university, one enrolled in the sociology department (or faculty) and studied political sociology. The political science faculty (if there was one) generally taught courses in political philosophy, international law, and after World War II, constitutional law, and sometimes even public administration and law[6]—all deductive, normative, and only incidentally empirical.

Political science as we know it today was pioneered and developed almost exclusively by universities and scholars in the United States. They got their initial impetus from European theorists and methodologists of history, sociology, and "political economy" (economics), but the realization of the goal of a science of politics distinct from sociology, philosophy, history or law, occurred in this country rather than Europe.

The whole movement toward graduate education in the United States took place after the Civil War, when many of our scholars went to German universities to study medicine, law, and eventually the social sciences.[7] The education which these universities gave their students was superior to that of similar institutions in the United States because of their emphasis on research as an integral part of their training.

One such student, John W. Burgess, on returning to this country succeeded in establishing the first graduate school in political science at Columbia University in 1880. The curriculum was broadly interdisciplinary, including economics, history, politics, geography, political theory, statistics, bibliography, and, in 1891, sociology. It also included courses in public law and jurisprudence,

---

6. Most of these courses, however, were taught by the law faculties before 1945.

7. What follows is largely an adaptation of the discussion to be found in *The Development of Political Science* by Albert Somit and Joseph Tanenhaus (Boston: Allyn and Bacon, 1967).

but with the theoretical and philosophical emphases so often lacking in our business-oriented law schools. The methodology of most of these offerings was comparative, with a heavy emphasis on research and the careful examination of facts, the use of logic to derive causal relationships from them, and "theory building." In many ways, therefore, the educational aims and methodology of the graduate curriculum of the first department of political science in the United States was not too much different from those which we find in the graduate schools today.

Before long other graduate departments of political science were established throughout the country, and this discipline (as well as others in the social sciences) soon found itself flourishing with sufficient vigor to allow the growth of an independent professional association and the proliferation of scholarly journals. In 1903 the American Political Science Association was founded, and three years later began publishing its *Review*.

Almost from the beginning, however, American political scientists found themselves differing over how to define the scope and purpose of their discipline, what their major concerns should be, and what methodologies should be used. Definitions of the discipline ranged all the way from "contemporary history" to "the science of the state." W. W. Willoughby divided political science into three areas: "the determination of fundamental philosophical principles . . . the description of political institutions or governmental organizations considered at rest, and . . . the determination of the laws of political life and development, the motives that give rise to political action, the conditions that occasion particular political manifestations . . ."[8]

The strongest advocate of the scientific approach to political science was John Burgess, its founder. He too saw three divisions within political science: political science proper (dealing with what we would call the political community), constitutional law (the regime and rules of the game), and public law (legislation and policies of particular administrations). And while he believed that political science could not be separated from history, he also held that there existed fundamental laws governing the growth and behavior of political institutions which comparative analysis could reveal, and that systematic theory based on a clear understanding of these three subdivisions could be built and used to predict outcomes of specific courses of policy.[9]

---

8. Quoted in Somit and Tanenhaus, *The Development of Political Science*, p. 25.
9. Ibid., p. 28.

Others like Munroe Smith and Jesse Macy also held to a scientific approach to politics, but the methodology to be used was not at all clear. In time, the historical-comparative method won out, since it was the most widely developed and simplest to use. Documents rather than personal or controlled observations became the main source of data for political science, and therefore history rather than sociology was considered its closest relative. Not long afterward, however, several "realists" like Woodrow Wilson revolted against "document rummaging" and opted instead for personal observation. This, plus the fact that the new students of politics were as yet not sufficiently socialized to the value-free role of the scientist, caused many of the early journals of political science to begin to resemble popular journals of opinion, dealing with contemporary political events[10] rather than with "laws" of political behavior.

American political science was unique among all the social science disciplines in that it assumed for itself the responsibility for educating the nation's youth for citizenship and participation in public affairs. Belief in American democracy, patriotism, and the rights and duties of citizens was to be carefully inculated among the young, many of whom were to be trained for leadership positions in government and other walks of public life. On this point there appeared to be virtual unanimity. Inherent in this position was the belief that the pursuit of scientific truth and the propagation of democratic values and practices could not be opposed, since, as Somit and Tanenhaus put it, ". . . it was obvious to all right-thinking men that democracy was the best and highest form of government . . ."[11] That the goals of scientific objectivity and citizenship education might indeed come into conflict did not occur to leaders in the profession until many years later, and the dichotomy is still very much with us today.

Despite the call for the "historical-comparative" approach and deductive theory building by the early "scientists," and the demand for personal observation and even participation by the "realists," the dominant mode of political inquiry in the early days of American political science, for some reason, consisted merely of ". . . routine description and pedestrian analysis of formal political structures and processes based on the more readily accessible official sources and records."[12] James Bryce's call for the "facts,

---

10. Ibid., p. 84.
11. Ibid., p. 48.
12. Ibid., p. 70.

facts, facts!" was misinterpreted to mean that political scientists should eschew theory and concentrate on simple description as their main research aim, and for a while political science did indeed appear to be going nowhere. There were some important exceptions, of course, and A. Lawrence Lowell, the fifth president of the American Political Science Association, was one. His presidential address condemned both the hyperfactualism of the then current variety of political research, and the overly-normative concerns of the discipline as well. He called for a wider use of statistics and quantitative data and for an expansion of the scope of research into non-public agencies, organizations and clubs, in order to understand politics in its broader sense. He has been accordingly ranked as the "intellectual godfather"[13] of the current behavioral movement, but unfortunately made little dent in the ongoing practices of his contemporaries.

Another exception was Arthur Bentley. In 1908 his *The Process of Government*[14] argued strenuously for what might today be called the "sociological" or "group" approach to political science. Claiming that political science at that time was dead because it ignored the central core of politics—activity as conducted by political groups (interest or "pressure" groups)—Bentley proposed, in a manner that reminded one of a nineteenth century proponent of Newtonian mechanics, that groups were that unit of politics which could best be quantified and whose interactions most resembled the molecules or units of the hard sciences. But while some reviewers of the book thought it had merit, the profession as a whole ignored it. It remained for David Truman[15] to review and adapt it forty years later for a discipline newly awakened to the changes that had occurred in its sister social sciences and only then ready to commence building a "scientific" political science in earnest.

To quote Somit and Tanenhaus again, the work of political scientists in the early days of the discipline, ". . . tended to be legalistic, descriptive, formalistic, conceptually barren, and largely devoid of what would today be called empirical data."[16] Institutional description replaced analytic conceptualization; comparative data were used as illustrations only, rather than for

---

13. Ibid., p. 74.
14. An excellent excerpt of the book is to be found in Heinz Eulau, Samuel J. Eldersveld, and Morris Janowitz, eds., *Political Behavior* (Glencoe, Ill.: The Free Press, 1956), pp. 14-24. The book was also re-issued by Harvard University Press in 1967.
15. *The Governmental Process* (New York: Alfred A. Knopf, 1951).
16. *The Development of Political Science*, p. 69.

systematic analysis and the formulation of "rules" of political behavior; "laws of politics" were abandoned as impractical; and the term "science" meant little more than traditional, serious scholarship. So far, in fact, had the political science profession departed from the original aims of Burgess, its founder, that in 1913 a report on political science instruction in colleges and universities by the Haines Committee of the American Political Science Association listed the following educational priorities: "1) to train for citizenship; 2) to prepare for professions such as law, journalism, teaching, and public service; 3) to train experts and to prepare specialists for government positions;" and, as an afterthought, "for the universities a fourth group might be added including courses primarily intended to train for research work."[17]

This situation did not remain unchallenged for long, however. In 1921 Charles E. Merriam launched the attack with a call for a "new science" of politics to be realized mainly through the use of techniques developed in psychology and statistics. He did not believe the elimination of the historical-comparative and legalistic approaches to the discipline should be attempted, but that precise measurement and testing of the insights which the older approaches provided was necessary. The main purpose of this "new science" was, as he put it, "more intelligent control of the process of government," "the elimination of waste in political action," the avoidance or minimization of war, revolutions, and "the imperfect adjustment of individuals and classes"[18]—in other words, the output of "scientific" policy. Far from being a proponent of scientific objectivity, therefore, Merriam believed that the new science of politics should serve democracy; it might be methodologically neutral, but its aim was public policy in the service of humanity.

Other advocates of scientific politics, like William Bennett Munro and G. E. G. Catlin, did not agree. Munro felt that the search for fundamental laws of political behavior should be the first aim, and scientific objectivity a major goal. Catlin even attempted a general theory of politics based on classical economics: instead of "economic man" motivated by the desire for wealth, he posited "political man" motivated by the desire for power. The unit of measurement he proposed in place of currency was, for the lack of anything more reliable, the vote, but he expressed the hope that

---

17. Quoted by Somit and Tanenhaus, *The Development of Political Science*, pp. 82-83.

18. Ibid., p. 111.

more suitable measures of political support might later be developed. However, Catlin was no more successful than Bentley had been in trying to convert the discipline to his theoretical framework.

But Charles Merriam did succeed in getting many of his ideas accepted by the American Political Science Association. At his urging the Association established a Committee on Political Research and held three National Conferences on the Science of Politics, which led ultimately to the founding of the very influential Social Science Research Council. For three years (1923-25) some of the best brains in the association met together with psychologists and statisticians to discuss the establishment of a science of politics, and the methodology and techniques required to accomplish it. The original goal under Merriam's leadership was still applied or policy science, however, and not pure science. But by the end of the three conferences the emphasis shifted to a "drive toward objectivity" as the "chief hope for the future of science."[19]

Following the conferences, a series of outstanding studies were published in the scientific mode, many of which are still considered classics. Works by Stuart A. Rice and Harold Lasswell established the feasibility of the use of quantitative techniques and insights from clinical psychology in political research, and Catlin's emphasis on the vote led to a series of voting studies based on the use of surveys rather than aggregate data. As a result, the University of Chicago, Merriam's home base, was established as the national center for the scientific study of politics, and its graduates and associates became the chief source in later years for the development of the behavioral movement. Among them were Lasswell himself, V. O. Key, Gabriel Almond, Leonard White, C. Herman Pritchett, Herbert Simon, Avery Leiserson and David Truman.

This revolt of the scientists did not sustain itself for very long, however. In 1927 the Association's Committee on Policy was established with Thomas H. Reed at its head, financed by enormous grants from the Carnegie Foundation. Its main aim appeared to be the re-orientation of the discipline away from science and back again toward citizenship education and training for public service. It tried to open the Association to the public at large, soliciting high school civics instructors and teachers colleges—but with little success. The committee was dissolved in 1935, but its activities served to demonstrate that there was no consensus among political

---

19. Quoted by Somit and Tanenhaus, ibid., p. 125.

scientists at that time as to the major aims and purposes of the discipline. However, its 1930 report did indicate some evidence of the effect of the scientific movement on the discipline. Instead of reproducing the 1913 Haines Committee's priority listing which had placed citizenship education first and research last, the Reed report interestingly enough reversed the order, placing research first, publication second, and citizenship education and training for public service last.[20]

The scientific movement became quiescent, however, as the nation found itself faced by two major political convulsions—the Depression and World War II. In the face of these overwhelming crises, few political scientists could maintain any semblance of scientific objectivity, and many soon found themselves competing for jobs in that same public service which they had earlier attempted to downgrade. Rumblings against the heavily descriptive and non-theoretical nature of much of the research being done by political scientists, and dissatisfaction with its "middle class" bias and lack of questioning of its overly-normative, democratic ideology, began to be heard in the 1940s despite these enormous crises. Robert D. Leigh, among others, led the way with his warning in 1944 that the meager "quantity of scientific content accumulated in our field" left political scientists open to the "danger of being exposed as quacks."[21]

After 1945, with the return of many political scientists to the groves of academe from their sometimes disillusioning experiences in government, the onslaughts on the inadequacies of the traditional approaches to the discipline—mainly the historical, the philosophical and the legal—began in earnest. In 1950 Lasswell and Kaplan outlined a theoretical framework for the study of power;[22] in 1951 David Truman published his adaptation of Bentley's thesis; and in 1953 David Easton's *The Political System*[23] drove home, as powerfully as anything could, the barrenness of hyperfactualism and the failure of contemporary political science to build anything resembling coherent theories of politics or to develop systematic techniques for gathering and analyzing data, with which such theories might be constructed. By mid-decade the term "behavioralism" (an adaptation of a similar term used in

---

20. Ibid., p. 132.

21. Quoted by Somit and Tanenhaus, ibid., p. 130.

22. Harold D. Lasswell and Abraham Kaplan, *Power and Society* (New Haven: Yale University Press, 1950).

23. (New York: Alfred A. Knopf, 1953).

psychology) was being used to describe the new movement toward a science of politics, as Harold Lasswell became president-elect of the American Political Science Association, and a flood of exhortatory as well as explanatory articles poured forth from the pens of behavioralism's many followers.

After much discussion and debate, David Easton finally published a list of those assumptions and objectives, the "intellectual foundation stones"[24] as he called them, of the new movement—an account which is considered to be the most reliable among the many which were written.[25] They are as follows:

(1) Regularities: There are discoverable uniformities in political behavior. These can be expressed in generalizations or theories with explanatory and predictive value.

(2) Verification: The validity of such generalizations must be testable, in principle, by reference to relevant behavior.

(3) Techniques: Means for acquiring and interpreting data cannot be taken for granted. They are problematic and need to be examined self-consciously, refined and validated so that rigorous means can be found for observing, recording, and analyzing behavior.

(4) Quantification: Precision in the recording of data and the statement of findings require measurement and quantification, not for their own sake, but only where possible, relevant, and meaningful in the light of other objectives.

(5) Values: Ethical evaluation and empirical explanation involve two different kinds of propositions that, for the sake of clarity, should be kept analytically distinct. However, a student of political behavior is not prohibited from asserting propositions of either kind separately or in combination as long as he does not mistake one for the other.

(6) Systematization: Research ought to be systematic; that is to say, theory and research are to be seen as closely intertwined parts of a coherent and orderly body of knowledge. Research untutored by theory may prove trivial, and theory unsupportable by data, futile.

---

24. "The Current Meaning of 'Behavioralism' in Political Science," *The Limits of Behavioralism in Political Science,* ed. James C. Charlesworth (Philadelphia: The American Academy of Political and Social Science, October, 1962), pp. 1-25. Used by permission of the author and the publisher.

25. See for example the treatment by Evron Kirkpatrick in "The Impact of the Behavioral Approach in Traditional Political Science," in Austin Ranney's *Essays on the Behavioral Study of Politics* (Urbana, Ill.: University of Illinois Press, 1962) pp. 1-29, and the Somit and Tanenhaus version of the behavioral "paradigm," *The Development of Political Science,* pp. 177-79.

(7) Pure science: The application of knowledge is as much a part of the scientific enterprise as theoretical understanding. But the understanding and explanation of political behavior logically precede and provide the basis for efforts to utilize political knowledge in the solution of urgent practical problems of society.

(8) Integration: Because the social sciences deal with the whole human situation, political research can ignore the findings of other disciplines only at the peril of weakening the validity and undermining the generality of its own results. Recognition of this interrelationship will help to bring political science back to its status of earlier centuries and return it to the main fold of the social sciences.

In addition to the call for placing pure science ahead of applied science and the emphasis on value-neutral research—two points of difference from the Merriam-sponsored movement—it is important also to note that the post-World War II development stressed the search for "regularities" expressed as "generalizations or theories with explanatory and predictive value" instead of "laws," thus demonstrating that the impact which relativity had had on epistemology in general had not been lost on the new behavioralists.

The fact, too, that Easton's final point argues on behalf of the interdisciplinary approach and the "return" of political science to the "main fold of the social sciences" would seem to indicate a desire to take up where Burgess had left off, and perhaps even to place a bit of the onus for having "left the fold" upon the much-castigated traditionalists. In any event, the divergence of political science away from the paths laid down by Burgess and the other "scientists" is treated as an unhealthy abberation—a refusal to take advantage of the new developments in social science methodology and technology which even Aristotle would not have ignored, had he been alive in the twentieth century.[26]

By 1961, the onslaught of the "Young Turks" against the strongholds of traditionalism was believed to have been so successful that Robert A. Dahl ventured (perhaps prematurely) to write what he called an "Epitaph for a Monument to a Successful Protest."[27] By that time a whole series of substantial studies utilizing the new techniques had been published, and foundation

---

26. See Heinz Eulau, *The Behavioral Persuasion in Politics* (New York: Random House, 1963), pp. 31-35, on this point.

27. "The Behavioral Approach in Political Science . . . ," *American Political Science Review* 55 (December 1961): 763-72.

money was flowing in to those centers and individuals engaging in behavioral research (among them perhaps the most outstanding is the Inter-university Consortium for Political Research of the Survey Research Center at the University of Michigan), including money and recognition eventually coming from the National Science Foundation itself. Shortly thereafter, the great majority of the officers and leaders of the American Political Science Association, as well as the greater number of articles published by the Association's *Review,* all indicated the preponderance of influence being exercised on the Association and the discipline by the new behavioralists.

This development did not go completely unchallenged, however. In 1960 Bernard Crick's study of *The American Science of Politics*[28] led the way with an Englishmen's jaundiced view of the movement, and in 1962 Leo Strauss, the outstanding proponent of the classical normative philosophical approach in America, together with some of his students and associates at the University of Chicago, launched a rather bitter attack on behavioralism in Herbert J. Storing's *Essays on the Scientific Study of Politics.*[29] Lasswell and others who were particularly singled out for criticism declined to reply, but two younger normative theorists, hardly likely to be classified as behavioralists themselves, did so.[30] The controversy rankled and erupted into some ugly scenes at several conventions of the Association, but the changes called for by the behavioralists were not at all slow in coming. In fact many political scientists who had received their basic training as traditionalists soon found that they would have to "re-tool" if they were to participate in very many of the conventions of the Association, or have their work published within the pages of the now prestigious *Review.* The change was an extraordinarily rapid one under the circumstances, and its repercussions were felt throughout the decade. However, by the end of the sixties behavioralism did triumph in American political science, but it also saw the beginning of another movement growing out of behavioralism itself, and questioning the very direction in which behavioralism and the profession were heading.

At the 1969 convention of the American Political Science Association, David Easton, this time in his capacity as President of

---

28. (Berkeley and Los Angeles: University of California Press, 1960).

29. (New York: Holt, Rinehard and Winston, 1962),

30. John H. Schaar and Sheldon S. Wolin, "Essays on the Scientific Study of Politics: A Critique," *American Political Science Review* 57 (March 1963): 125-50. See also the "Replies to Schaar and Wolin" by Storing, Strauss, *et al,* ibid., pp. 151-60.

the Association, called the attention of the profession to "The New Revolution in Political Science"[31] which was presently taking place. Categorizing it as "post-behavioralism," its battle cries were "relevance" and "action." Easton listed seven tenets of what he called its "Credo of Relevance":

1. Substance must precede technique. If one must be sacrificed for the other—and this need not always be so—it is more important to be relevant and meaningful for contemporary urgent social problems than to be sophisticated in the tools of investigation. For the aphorism of science that it is better to be wrong than vague, post-behavioralism would substitute a new dictum, that it is better to be vague than non-relevantly precise.

2. Behavioral science conceals an ideology of empirical conservatism. To confine oneself exclusively to the description and analysis of facts is to hamper the understanding of these same facts in their broadest context. As a result empirical political science must lend its support to the maintenance of the very factual conditions it explores. It unwittingly purveys an ideology of social conservation tempered by modest incremental change.

3. Behavioral research must lose touch with reality. The heart of behavioral inquiry is abstraction and analysis and this serves to conceal the brute realities of politics. The task of post-behavioralism is to break the barriers of silence that behavioral language necessarily has created and to help political science reach out to the real needs of mankind in a time of crisis.

4. Research about and constructive development of values are inextinguishable parts of the study of politics. Science cannot be and never has been evaluatively neutral despite protestations to the contrary. Hence to understand the limits of our knowledge we need to be aware of the value premises on which it stands and the alternatives for which this knowledge could be used.

5. Members of a learned discipline bear the responsibilities of all intellectuals. The intellectuals' historical role has been and must be to protect the humane values of civilization. This is their unique task and obligation. Without this they become mere technicians, mechanics for tinkering with society. They thereby abandon the special privileges they have come to claim for themselves in academia, such as freedom of inquiry and a quasi-extraterritorial protection from the onslaughts of society.

6. To know is to bear the responsibility for acting and to act is to engage in reshaping society. The intellectual as scientist bears

---

31. *American Political Science Review* 63 (December 1969): 1051-61. Used by permission of the author and the publisher.

the special obligation to put his knowledge to work. Contemplative science was a product of the nineteenth century when a broader moral agreement was shared. Action science of necessity reflects the contemporary conflict in society over ideals and this must permeate and color the whole research enterprise itself.

7. If the intellectual has the obligation to implement his knowledge, those organizations composed of intellectuals—the professional associations—and the universities themselves, cannot stand apart from the struggles of the day. Politicization of the professions is inescapable as well as desirable.

The post-behavioral revolution had come, therefore, not to destroy the scientific impetus of behavioralism,[32] but to awaken its practitioners to the needs of the times and to their obligations toward their fellow men, and to encourage them to use their expertise to help solve the social and political problems which the sixties had revealed in all their gory ugliness. The ethical neutrality of the scientist was a "cop-out,"[33] some said—a means of supporting the conservative forces of society which favored the status quo. Political scientists should be helping to construct alternative models of political society instead of withdrawing from the battle. Applied research is the immediate need of the discipline, not basic research which takes too long to come to fruition. The problems which cry out for solution are here and now, and cannot wait for the slow wheels of science to grind out the final answers. Politicization of the profession is called for, because knowledge imposes the duty

---

32. There is some question of the validity of this interpretation. According to Eugene F. Miller ("Positivism, Historicism, and Political Inquiry," *APSR* 72: 796-817) the post-behavioralists are really opposed to the entire behavioralist or scientific enterprise in political science because of their basic opposition to the empiricist tradition on which its epistemology is based. They are instead, historicists, or epistemological relativists who deny that valid knowledge of reality, much less progress, in science is possible, since all knowledge is historically or culturally determined. In Miller's view the aims of the post-behavioralists cannot be reconciled with the efforts of the behavioralists to make political science "scientific," since they are opposed to "science" as behavioralists and logical positivists have defined it. Comments on Miller's article in the same edition of *APSR* indicate considerable dissent, on the part of the behavioralists and philosophers of science who responded, from Miller's interpretations of the current beliefs and practices of behavioralists and positivists. There did not appear to be any dissent from his view of the epistemological position of the post-behavioralists, however. If his interpretation on this point is correct, then it would be best to separate the views of the policy scientists per se from those of the post-behavioralists. The latter would appear to be primarily interested in changing society through "radical" goal-directed policy, while the former, going back to the tradition of Merriam, would wish to concentrate upon the development of policy by scientific means.

33. Author's phrase, not Easton's.

of service—to all mankind and not just to the elites of society, the government, business, those military and voluntary associations which can pay for our expertise. Easton continues:

> In accepting this new (but ancient) obligation of the intellectual, however, we need to recognize that the professional political scientist may engage in three distinguishable kinds of activity. These are teaching and research on the one hand and practical politics on the other. Somewhere between these the political scientist acts as a consultant and an adviser. Each of these kinds of activity—as a scholar, politician, and consultant—shapes and influences the other. Is it feasible to construct a single organization that will serve the collective purposes of the profession for facilitating all three of these kinds of activities? It seems highly unlikely. Can we provide some sensible division of labor among different organizations that will permit the fullest expression for all those activities into which these critical times are pressing the professional political scientist? This seems possible.[34]

Calling then for the establishment of a Federation of Social Scientists to "identify the major issues of the day, clarify objectives, evaluate action taken by others, study and propose alternative solutions, and press these vigorously in the political sphere;"[35] Easton in effect was proposing a continuation of the basic research aims of the behavioralists under the guise of the present American Political Science Association, but with a parallel organization or federation composed of members from all the social sciences to work in the area of applied science or policy.

The solution was not immediately accepted by the activist members of the American Political Science Association, however, and in the years which followed, the "Caucus for a New Political Science" attempted to re-orient the Association to its own views of the duties of the profession. But it would appear that well over two-thirds of the general membership prefer what has been called the "establishment" position of public non-partisanship for the Association in socially political matters, to the Caucus' call for involvement. This is the conclusion drawn by the Vice Chairman of the Caucus, Charles J. Fox, from his assessment of the results of the election of officers of the Association which took place by mail ballot following the 1970 convention.[36] The Caucus, which had

34. Ibid., p. 1060.
35. Ibid.
36. Charles J. Fox, "Democratic Elitism Close to Home," P. S. 4 (Spring 1971): 126-29.

enjoyed considerable panel space and sessions for the dissemination of its views at the 1970 convention, was denied the privilege of having any panels at all at the 1971 convention, by that same mail ballot.

An attempt on the part of the more conservative elements of the behavioral establishment to limit participation and membership in the Association to Ph.D.'s and those genuinely involved in academic life was defeated by the 1971 convention, but an article in the Summer 1972 edition of *P.S.*, the house organ of the APSA, clearly indicated that the behavioralists are in no immediate danger of being replaced by the members of the "radical" Caucus. According to a survey of political scientists in eight western states, fewer than one-fifth of those responding were in favor of the post-behavioralist position, while 40% were definitely opposed.[37] At the present time it appears a reasonable generalization to state that the post-behavioralists are in a distinct minority within the profession, and that its adherents can be elected to posts of influence within the Association only when sponsored by its leaders (mostly behavioralists) in the interest of democratic representation of all factions.

The future of the Caucus for a New Political Science is uncertain. Whether it will continue its efforts to re-orient the profession to political activism, or will instead take David Easton's advice and seek to establish some sort of Federation of Social Scientists through which to channel its interests, is not immediately known. However, two new journals whose primary aim is the sponsoring of research and discussion into policy concerns were launched in 1970, one of which, *Politics and Society,* numbers among its editors and advisors most of the published leaders of the Caucus, including Peter Bachrach, the Caucus' 1972 candidate for the presidency of the American Political Science Association.

Thus the battle has been joined, and which side will win—if either—will probably not be determined in one, two, or maybe five conventions. There is room within the profession, certainly, for both points of view. Whether the Association itself should be the instrument for policy development and partisanship on political issues is another matter entirely. But behavioralism per se, the use of scientific methodology as the principal means of political

---

37. Kendall L. Baker, Sami J. Hajjar, Alan Evan Schenker, "Note on Behavioralists and Post-Behavioralists in Contemporary Political Science," *P. S.* (Summer 1972): 271-73.

inquiry, appears to be in possession of the fortress at the present time, and it will probably take a considerably stronger siege than the Caucus has yet been able to mount to cause it to be dislodged in the near or immediately forseeable future.[38]

---

38. Michael Haas and Theodore L. Becker have proposed a "multimethodological" approach combining the historical (unique, case-study) and philosophical concerns of the traditionalists, with the theoretical and positivist ("brute" empirical) concerns of the behavioralists. Their point is that a concentration on any one of the eight items of the behavioral "creed," as stated by Easton, weakens the scientific endeavor; and that an amalgam of approaches is better than the dichotomy which presently exists between the theorists (traditional and behavioral) and the empiricists. "A Multimethodological Plea," *Polity* 2 (Spring 1970): 267-94. A similar position is taken by Heinz Eulau, except that he still sees the search for the absolute answers of the classical traditionalists to be at the core of the discipline—a view somewhat at variance with the current scientific concept of reality. "Tradition and Innovation: On the Tension between Ancient and Modern Ways in the Study of Politics," *Behavioralism in Political Science* (New York: Atherton Press, 1969), pp. 1-121.

Suggested Readings

Baker, Kendall L., Sami J. Hajjar, and Alan Evan Schenker. "Note on Behavioralists and Post-Behavioralists in Contemporary Political Science." *P.S.* 5 (Summer, 1972): 271-73.

Becker, Howard and Harry Elmer Barnes. *Social Thought From Lore to Science,* 3d ed. 3 vols. New York: Dover, 1961.

Bentley, Arthur F. *The Process of Government.* Cambridge, Mass.: Harvard University Press, 1967.

Braybrooke, David and Alexander Rosenberg. "Comment: Getting the War News Straight: The Actual Situation in the Philosophy of Science." *APSR* 66 (September 1972): 818-26.

Charlesworth, James C., ed. *The Limits of Behavioralism in Political Science.* Philadelphia: The American Academy of Political and Social Science, October 1962.

Crick, Bernard. *The American Science of Politics, Its Origins and Conditions.* Berkeley and Los Angeles: University of California Press, 1960.

Dahl, Robert A. "The Behavioral Approach in Political Science: Epitaph for a Monument to a Successful Protest." *APSR* 55 (December, 1961): 763-72.

Duverger, Maurice. *An Introduction to the Social Sciences.* New York: Praeger, 1964.

Easton, David. "The Current Meaning of 'Behavioralism' in Political Science." In *The Limits of Behavioralism in Political Science,* edited by James C. Charlesworth, pp. 1-25. Philadelphia: The American Academy of Political and Social Science, October 1962.

Easton, David. "The New Revolution in Political Science." *APSR* 63 (December, 1969): 1051-61.

Easton, David. *The Political System,* 2d ed. New York: Knopf, 1971.

Eulau, Heinz. *The Behavioral Persuasion in Politics.* New York: Random House, 1963.

Eulau, Heinz. "Tradition and Innovation: On the Tension Between Ancient and Modern Ways in the Study of Politics." In *Behavioralism in Political Science,* edited by Heinz Eulau, pp. 1-21. New York: Atherton Press, 1969.

Haas, Michael. "The Rise of a Science of Politics." *Approaches to the Study of Political Science,* edited by Michael Haas and Henry S. Kariel, pp. 3-48. Scranton, Pa.: Chandler, 1970.

Haas, Michael and Theodore L. Becker. "The Behavioral Revolution and After." *Approaches to the Study of Political Science,* edited by Michael Haas and Henry S. Kariel, pp. 479-510. Scranton, Pa.: Chandler, 1970.

Haas, Michael and Theodore L. Becker. "A Multimethodological Plea." *Polity* 2 (Spring, 1970): 267-94.

Kirkpatrick, Evron. "The Impact of the Behavioral Approach in Traditional Political Science." In *Essays on the Behavioral Study of Politics,* edited by Austin Ranney, pp. 1-29. Urbana: University of Illinois Press, 1962.

Kuhn, Thomas S. *The Structure of Scientific Revolutions.* Chicago: University of Chicago Press, 1962.

Miller, Eugene F. "Positivism, Historicism, and Political Inquiry." *APSR* 66 (September, 1972): 796-817.

Miller, Eugene F. "Rejoinder to 'Comments' by David Braybrooke and Alexander Rosenberg, Richard S. Rudner and Martin Landau." *APSR* 66 (September, 1972): 857-73.

Osgood, Charles E. "Behavior Theory and the Social Sciences." In *Contemporary Analytical Theory,* edited by David E. Apter and Charles F. Andrain, pp. 495-518. Englewood Cliffs, N. J.: Prentice-Hall, 1972.

Ranney, Austin. "The Study of Policy Content: A Framework for Choice." In *Political Science and Public Policy,* edited by Austin Ranney, pp. 3-21. Chicago: Markham, 1968.

Schaar, John H., and Sheldon S. Wolin. "Essays on the Scientific Study of Politics: A Critique." *APSR* 57 (March 1963): 125-50.

Somit, Albert and Joseph Tanenhaus. *The Development of Political Science.* Boston: Allyn and Bacon, 1967.

Storing, Herbert J., ed. *Essays on the Scientific Study of Politics.* New York: Holt, Rinehart and Winston, 1962.

Strauss, Leo. "What is Political Philosophy? The Problem of Political Philosophy." In *Behavioralism in Political Science,* edited by Heinz Eulau, pp. 93-108. New York: Atherton Press, 1969.

Truman, David B. "The Impact on Political Science of the Revolution in the Behavioral Sciences." In *Behavioralism in Political Science,* edited by Heinz Eulau, pp. 38-67. New York: Atherton Press, 1969.

Voegelin, Eric. *The New Science of Politics, An Introduction.* Chicago: University of Chicago Press, 1952.

CHAPTER VII

Science and Values

We come now to discuss one of the knottiest problems in philosophical inquiry. A matter of special concern to the social sciences in general, to political science it is the most central of all the issues which seek for solution at the present time: the question of values and the role which science can play in clarifying and rationalizing decisions. We have placed the discussion of this problem almost at the end of the book so that the student will have had the opportunity to review the history of the discipline and to become familiar with the current rift between the behavioralists and the post-behavioralists before becoming too deeply enmeshed in the intricacies of the philosophical problem of values and value theory. The present controversy in political science only serves to accentuate the importance of this question to our discipline and to demonstrate with singular clarity the centrality of values for political scientists in general.

Traditional political theory (philosophical, not empirical theory as we now know it) was mainly deductive and normative in character. Its principal purpose was to determine the rationally best or ideal state (usually by philosophical insight or intuition á la Plato), and to infer from such a determination how the state should be run, the obligations of each component of this ideal socio-political system to every other component and to the whole, as well

103

as the obligations of the whole to each of its parts and to its equals in the international arena.

Moralistic and legalistic in orientation, traditional political theory attempted to determine how the citizen as well as the state should behave in the ideal moral, legal and political situation. Deviations from the ideal were condemned as immoral or in violation of some principle of natural, divine, or international law, and very often served to justify revolutions, wars, insurgencies, and in some instances, regicide (usually called tyrannicide). They also served to justify repressions of insurgencies, counterrevolutions, wars of deterrence and preventive wars, invasions, the mass persecutions and/or slaughterings of political deviants, rebels (traitors), and hostages—all in the name of the "right" or "good" state or political system (Republicanism, Democracy, Divine Right, Socialism, Fascism, etc.).

Everyone who acted in the political arena claimed to be acting in the name of Justice or Freedom, on behalf of Equality or Humanity, or for God, the Church, the Crown, the Flag, the Republic, or simply the People. No one would admit to self-interest as his, his nation's, or his faction's primary motivation: idealized values of one sort or another were always put forth as the "real" reason for engaging in the political activity of the moment.

Political theory, therefore, frequently served no other immediate purpose than to justify or rationalize political decisions, and in this sense was indistinguishable from political ideology. When it did attempt to deal dispassionately with the "eternal" question of man's relationship to man in political society, it did come closer to the ideal of speculative philosophy, but seldom was any author able to divorce himself from his own political background and biases sufficiently to enable him to perceive and to restrain the expression of his own cultural and personal value systems.

In the nineteenth and twentieth centuries, however, this problem of values and of value perspectives came to be recognized and dealt with in several different ways. Hegel posited a dialectical movement between contradictory value systems which eventually would result in an historically determined synthesis or resolution of the problem; Marx saw Communism as the final or "right" historical solution; historicism gave rise to cultural relativism (to each his own, so to speak); while science (or scientism), speaking through some of the analytic proponents of philosophy and logical positivism (philosophers of science), took the attitude of "A pox on all your houses!" To the positivists, values were just emotional preferences—outside the realm of reason and of science, and therefore, of little consequence, if not meaningless to scientists. They could only harm, not help, the scientific enterprise. They were to be denounced, eschewed, and if possible, outlawed. Science should in all things be "value free" (itself a value judgment).

But it wasn't long before science, and the social sciences especially, began to realize the impossibility of the last injunction. Every scientific activity is enframed in values and motivated by value judgments. Is it simply an "emotional preference" to decide to survive rather than die, to go to the moon, to battle cancer or try to prevent an economic depression, to fight racial segregation or the denial of civil liberties? Surely some if not all of these have a high rational as well as an emotional content. Every decision one makes, even the decision to engage in scientific research, involves a value judgment. Are all such judgements to be considered purely emotional?

The character of values and of value judgments has been debated endlessly over the last few decades. Max Weber felt that the "is" and the "ought" (facts and values) should be kept separate, and that scientific methodology could only be applied to facts. But the increasing recognition of the rational and factual elements in value judgments has led to great changes in the way in which values and value judgments have been treated in science and scientific philosophy in general.

One of the reasons for this change in outlook is that Mannheim's response to relativity theory and cultural relativism is at last beginning to have its effect on normative and ethical speculation. Also, social forces apparently at work in contemporary society are pressuring all of the social sciences to examine the problem of norms and values in a pluralistic environment. In fact, the social sciences are today being urged to view themselves as that branch of human knowledge which is uniquely concerned with values—how they evolve, are established and implemented, conflict and change, and how they color every aspect of interpersonal relations, political as well as social and moral. Their concern is not so much with how individuals and societies should behave under certain circumstances—this is still the realm of ethics and value theory per se—but why individuals and societies behave as they do, how their value systems come to differ or resemble each other, and how values and value judgments come into being. The exceptions, of course, are the policy scientists, the post-behavioralists. They would like to establish an ethics of government and of society—to use science to establish norms of political and social behavior and to determine policy that is "good" for mankind and society in general.

Political science has long been considered the study of "Who gets what, when and how"[1] and "the authoritative allocation of values for a society."[2] What men want, need, desire or prefer are, of course, what they value—their interests, to use political jargon. Value judgments are expressions of value preferences or decisions. Norms are standards of behavior dictated by or inferred from value judgments, and may be either individual or social. When social in extent they are frequently devised to secure to each individual as much of those values as his society believes he has coming to him: he ought or ought not to do thus and so, because a violation of that norm will upset the delicate balance which exists between social and individual value expectations and payoffs. "Thou shalt not kill" may be a Divine Commandment, but it is also a norm designed to stabilize the social order. If it is not generally adhered to by all or the great majority of the members of a particular society, and if they do not universally condemn and seek to eliminate all deliberate violations of that norm as they interpret it, then the maintenance of that society may become extremely difficult and its pattern of value allocations disrupted.

Culture is composed of, among other things, those patterns of norms and values which are considered proper and right by a particular society—the expectations of that society. Governments, at least since the days of the great Depression, have come to be considered the major value-distributing and norm-setting (as well as goal-achieving) agencies for societies. Public policy, sometimes in the form of legislation, is the end product of a particular society's political deliberations and processes—the actual decisions by which the available values are distributed among the demanding, supporting, and often conflicting elements of that society's citizenry. Law is both the means by which values are distributed and the public promulgation of the norms of behavior which the

---

1. Part of a book title by Harold Lasswell, *Politics: Who Gets What, When, How* (reissued by Meridian Books, New York, 1958).

2. David Easton, *The Political System* (New York: Alfred A. Knopf, 1953), p. 129. These are just two of many attempts to define political science and its subject matter, politics. No definition has been universally acclaimed as accurate or adequate by modern political scientists. The ones presented in this chapter are simply those which most clearly reveal the concern for values which has persisted in political science, even among its most outstanding behavioralists.

decision-making body or government of a society believes is necessary to the society's preservation and harmonious operation. As such law is the "score card" of the political struggle, recording the victories of the winning coalitions on each policy battle. It is for this reason that political science cannot ignore the question of values and must expend considerable effort in clarifying the processes and mechanisms by which values are generated and value judgments concluded.

Recent developments in ethics as well as in the social sciences point the way to the possible extension of scientific methodology to the question of values. In fact, decision theory and its many variations as developed in political science, mathematics, and the other social sciences (game theory, simulations, etc.), appears to be very closely related to the types of techniques which students of ethics are presently exploring in their attempts to solve the problem of rationality in the making of moral choices.

How one makes a decision, moral, political, social, or whatever, is no longer considered to be purely a matter of obeying authority, conscience, or revelation, of following hunches, insights, intuitions or emotions, or even of "upbringing." Rather it is an area into which reason and science must be allowed to extend their sway. What was once downgraded as an "emotional preference" might simply be the recognition of its lack of system and specificity due to insufficient data. Rationality can be inserted into the decision process, it is hoped, by the application of scientific techniques for the discovery of the factual and theoretical (explanatory) bases of correct or "wise" choices. If all the facts be known, if explanatory links can be established between actions and their consequences, then decisions can be made in a scientific manner. Once the payoffs have been measured and weighted, as in game theory, the rational (wise) decision is simply that which will result in the highest payoff (the greatest value). The calculus of choice, the rules governing the determination of weights for each payoff (the method by which they are ranked) reduces the decision to a simple matter of addition and subtraction: a computer could do it much more quickly and probably more efficiently than any one man or committee. The great problem, however, is that of determining the actual (ideal?) calculus of choice in any given situation—the dominant strategy for each player.

As persons familiar with game theory know, different outcomes may be ranked differently by different individuals. Thus one person may prefer outcome *B* to *A* to *D* to *C*, and another may rank his preferences *D, C, B, A*. Why each individual differs in the values he holds may depend upon many different circumstances, not the least of which may be irrational, unconscious drives as well as well-calculated payoffs and interests. The latter are considered to be rational, wise (clever?) reasons for choices; the former are not. Thus values come, in the pragmatic sense, to be considered instruments for the satisfaction of needs, conscious or unconscious. To ensure that a decision will be made scientifically requires that all one's reasons be fully probed and understood, and that the best way to achieve one's goals has been established factually by the discovery of the actual links between actions and their effects. In other words, scientific techniques can not only help to reveal one's true interests (values), they can also help one discover the best way to achieve them, and thereby further the rationalization of the decision process (the making of value judgments). Thus values and value judgments can no longer be treated as absolutes which bind and are the same for all men ("Thou shalt not . . ."), but rather as interests and decisions which are to be rationally calculated from known facts about the individual making the choice and the situation evoking it.

But what about social values and political value judgments? Values can no longer be treated as absolutes, but can they nevertheless be made to be binding on all persons in a society as fulfilling that society's needs, regardless of the many differing interests and needs of the individuals composing it? Is there some mechanism, in other words, which acts on values as scientific methodology does on facts? Can certain values be "validated" or "verified" for groups of individuals (or for the "human race") as facts can for scientists? Can value judgments bind or convince citizens as effectively as reliable experimental findings can persuade scientists?

It is at this point that Mannheim's solution begins to strike home. For if intersubjectivity works for facts, why not for values and norms? The essential difference between facts and values, the follower of Mannheim is likely to propose, appears to be the degree of consensus which each are able to evoke. If I say a pencil is red and you say it is blue, it is not too difficult to determine which one of us is factually correct. But if I say a painting of a Campbell's soup can is good art and you say it is trash, the only way for us to settle our differences is for each of us to list our reasons for saying so. In other words, the technique for establishing the validity of values is not all that different from the technique for establishing the validity of facts.[3] By listing our "reasons" we discover the differences in our value standards—why what is "good" for one can be "poison" for another. The problem then is to attempt some sort of consensus on our "reasons" and the order of importance which we give to each one. Value judgments, in other words, may be based on facts (line, color, composition) as well as emotional, cultural or psychological preferences. But while the factual components of our values may be operationalized and thus are, theoretically at least, scientifically verifiable, the psychological, emotional, subjective components may not always be.

We say "may not be" because we are not sure. Someday it may be possible for us to determine why it is that some people prefer pink kitchens to yellow ones, jazz to rock, croquet to frisbee, chess to checkers, democracy to communism. Pink may be calming and yellow exciting; jazz may express hope and rock anger; democracy may be a form of government which only the rich and secure find psychologically rewarding, and communism that of the frightened peasant. The subjective elements of value preferences, in other words, may be rooted in psychological predispositions and for this reason may never be universalizable as absolutes or near-absolutes (or verifiable as facts are) for large groups of individuals or "mankind" with any high degree of probability, even at a social or cultural level.

The distinction between fact and value, therefore, may remain the degree of consensus which each can attain. Facts are simple intellectual exercises in comparison with values. Until we can learn more about the social and psychological functions which values serve for societies and individuals, we shall never be able to understand them, much less "validate" them. The day when values become universal may be the day when men have become little more than homogenized duplicates of one another—psychologically as well as culturally. Thus Mannheim's solution, while scientifically valid, may be psychologically horrifying when applied to values. It may be a simple matter to establish social consensus on facts. The question is whether we can establish consensus on values, especially if consensus is construed for values as it is for facts, as somewhere in the range of 75% to 100% agreement, and scientific verification as possible at a mean standard error of 5% at the .05 level of confidence. Are these kinds of criteria, kinds which are most often treated as standard in science, at all possible of

---

3. See pp. 52-53, above.

application to values? Is a form of psychological as well as social and political totalitarianism implied in the very proposal? And if psychological predispositions contain physiological or genetic components, is the only hope for a universal value system the genetic as well as the social uniformity of the race?

The problem for moralists, value theorists, policy scientists, post-behavioralists, or all those who would hope to establish a single value herarchy for society or to ease the human condition through humane or progressive policy proposals, is an empirical one rather than a logical or a philosophical one. Not only must research into the extensiveness to which certain values are maintained be conducted (e.g., how widely held are the taboos against murder, incest, robbery, rape, slavery, gambling, homosexuality, abortion, premarital sex, etc.), but the relationship between values and their functions for individuals and societies must also be extensively explored. Investigations should try to determine under what conditions certain values will be held by certain individuals and societies, and what consequences for these individuals and societies each value judgment may have.[4] The question of verification or social validation of values, therefore, may never be any more than a matter of transitory, here-and-now, temporary agreement on a particular value position for this situation and for this situation only. If consensus does occur it could be more a matter of happenstance than of permanent acceptance of the "right." If political elections are any guidelines, so many extraneous factors can intervene to prevent or change a value consensus at any one time that any authoritative statement concerning what "the people want" can easily be reduced to so much verbal spaghetti. Value theory, in other words, may become empirical, and value science a distinct possibility, but millions of discrete items of information and explanatory hypotheses concerning the weight and distribution of causal factors (psychological, environmental, cultural, political, etc.) of every description will first have to be gathered, classified, elaborated and organized into a systematic theory of human behavior as it impinges on value choices and social decisions, before any such enterprise can hope to become as fruitful as we might wish. And grand theory, theory applicable to all mankind, may never be more than sweeping generalities of the type which are so broad as to be

---

4. For an impassioned discussion of the need to investigate the consequences of values, see Eugene J. Meehan, *The Foundations of Political Analysis, Empirical and Normative* (Homewood, Ill.: Dorsey Press, 1971), Part II.

next to meaningless in the concrete, and closer to rhetoric than science (e.g., "all men prefer freedom to slavery").

In the event that such an undertaking should get underway, political value theory may one day take its place beside what is presently called empirical theory in political science, since both will have thereby become empirical. The gap between the two will thus have ceased to exist. The major difference, however, between what we presently consider the task of value theory and its future task is the determination of what "should" be done in any particular instance. This last question, in its absolutist sense, has already become irrelevant, for not what "should" a society's goals eternally be, but rather what value configurations will arise in response to certain needs, psychological, political, or social, and *then* what alternative action prescriptions can the policy scientist or value theorist propose for the satisfaction of such needs. Thus the value scientist and the policy scientist will be able to work hand in hand, the first discovering the "laws" of value responses on a social level, and the second determining the most efficient paths by which to achieve each goal. "Should" therefore becomes reduced to a prescription for action rather than an absolute imperative. And the payoffs can then be rationally calculated even on a social level so that the choice itself becomes rational. Thus the question "What should our goals be," in an absolute sense, is replaced by the questions, "Under certain circumstances what should our goals be?" and "How are we most likely to attain them?" Probability theory is thus introduced into the equation and in this way logic and rationality are made an inherent part of the social value science (policy science) enterprise, as well as the science of individual ethics.

The deductive approach to value theory is not thereby completely invalidated. If one wishes to remain deductive rather than empirical in one's method, one could begin with a set of factual assumptions about the nature of man, his instinct for self-preservation, and thus his need for social institutions, as has been done by many philosophers in the past.[5] In conjunction with these factual assumptions one could also propose a series of assumptions about the needs, goals and interests which might be pursued by individuals and societies under certain circumstances. One might still proceed to deduce certain norms of behavior for achieving the

---

5. See Frederick M. Watkins, "Natural Law and the Problem of Value-Judgment," in Oliver Garceau, ed. *Political Research and Political Theory* (Cambridge, Mass.: Harvard University Press, 1968), pp. 58-74, for one such recent endeavor.

goals and maintaining the institutions which "man's nature" requires. But in doing so, one has still not solved the problem of validation of one's factual or value assumptions, or the verification of the causal linkages between the norms (prescriptions) and the goals they are proposed to achieve. The fact that many other sciences begin with certain assumptions, held in abeyance and just postulated until some solution can be worked out, may be considered sufficient justification for a value science doing the same thing. The difference is that in the purely empirical sciences many alternative models may be considered at the same time and tested empirically to see which one best conforms to reality as we can discover it. This is not, however, what was usually meant in the past when value theory was proposed as a solution to the question of norms. As we have already indicated, values and norms were traditionally interpreted to be absolutes which everyone should strive to achieve and maintain. In other words, "human nature" being the same for all men, their needs were the same and hence their values should also be the same.

But if one were willing to take the leap and make the quest for values and norms as tentative as most quests in science as a whole, and so postulate no definitive knowledge of what "human nature" (hence needs) is all about, then the deductive mode is not an entirely useless one. For then one could simply posit as many alternative models as one could devise, and proceed to test the consequences of each empirically for the best fit. In other words, one would merely be entering the scientific enterprise from the deductive end rather than the empirical one. The process of verification, however, would remain the same throughout, and a science of values would still be the end product.

But simply to assume certain "truths" to be "self-evident" and to deduce certain norms of behavior from them, postulated in an imperative or universal fashion, is a procedure which no longer has any validity—at least not for the social sciences. Such a procedure may still be valid in some theological or metaphysical enterprises, but not where one wishes to explain the actual differences which one sees among men, their societies and cultures, and their visible aspirations. Thus social science, as a value-conscious inquiry, calls out for the application of scientific procedures to even this last stronghold of the old philosophical mother-discipline. For as long as science remains empirically oriented and determined to push its knowledge of reality as far as it will go—to enlarge the realm of "fact" to its farthest possible frontiers—then values can no longer expect to remain untouched. For values themselves are today perceived by those of the scientific bent of mind to be little more than functional facts, instruments for the satisfaction of certain social, psychological, etc., needs.

As Dewey has already indicated, the difference between ends and means may simply be where one has left off in the ends-means chain. An end today may be tomorrow's means to another end. The problem is to discover the causal link—the link between the value judgment and its consequences, the way in which the value decision may actually resolve a need, whether perceived or not, and thus perform its hypothetical function. Once this has been done, of course, a vastly different type of value theory will have been constructed, and the dichotomy, presumably, between basic and applied science (the behavioralists and the policy scientists) in political science will also have been resolved. If value scientists are successful in their quest for understanding the functions which values perform, they will also have succeeded in placing *all* theory on a far firmer foundation than presently exists.

The policy scientist appears to be "at war" with the behavioralist more from a sense of urgency than from any disagreement over the need for basic research. The behavioralist, on the other hand, has a tendency to feel that applied science is for technicians and engineers rather than for "true" scientists. Presumably value science might be able to shed some light on the functions which these two conflicting value positions perform for the individuals involved, and even for the society they serve. There can be little doubt that both are needed *in* science and *by* society, for application is the "field-test" of science—the type that no laboratory or computer can provide. The problem is to get them both working together rather than each trying to dominate or convert the other. If each are made conscious of their motivations and the needed functions which their motivations serve, then hopefully tolerance and cooperation may replace conflict and anger.

In this light, value science may indeed be the first step in the direction of resolving all sorts of conflicts—political as well as social and psychological. Decisions will still have to be made, of course, as value allocation will still require some process or method of distribution. Politics will not cease to exist, but the understanding of the relationship between demands and functions which value science may provide could go a long way toward increasing the rationality of policy making in particular, and of all other types of value choices which men and societies encounter.

Value judgments will no longer be mysterious and arbitrary characteristics of human beings, but will have functional, if not rational, bases which all can understand. Thus by expanding the boundaries of human knowledge in this particular direction the value scientist may be able to diminish many of the areas of conflict which have so long plagued the human race.

It is very doubtful that conflict per se will ever be eliminated, for men will always differ socially, culturally and psychologically. But the effects of these differences may be easier to cope with once they are better understood. And values are just one of the many different classes of effects which may be studied from the scientific viewpoint. When that happens, science and values will no longer be at odds with each other. The "ought" will simply be another problematic hypothesis subject to testing and verification by the scientific method. And on that day philosophy and science may perhaps be united once again into one major all encompassing discipline. Defining wisdom to include its functional (instrumental, rational) element may become a respectable exercise among the moralists as well as among the scientists who search for "truth," and Machiavelli may one day be hailed as a pioneer in ethics for his elaboration of a political value theory suitable for sixteenth century Florence.

Suggested Readings

Bronowski, Jacob. *Science and Human Values.* Rev. ed. New York: Harper and Row, 1965.

Frohock, Fred M. *The Nature of Political Inquiry,* chapter five. Homewood, Ill.: Dorsey Press, 1967.

Lasswell, Harold D. *Politics: Who Gets What, When, How.* New York: Meridian Books, 1958.

Meehan, Eugene J. *The Foundations of Political Analysis, Empirical and Normative.* Homewood, Ill.: Dorsey Press, 1971.

Meehan, Eugene J. *Value Judgment and Social Science.* Homewood, Ill.: Dorsey Press, 1969.

Schelling, T. C. "What is Game Theory?" In *Contemporary Political Analysis,* edited by James C. Charlesworth, pp. 212-38. New York: Free Press, 1967.

Shubik, Martin. "The Uses of Game Theory." In *Contemporary Political Analysis,* edited by James C. Charlesworth, pp. 239-72. New York: Free Press, 1967.

Taylor, Paul W. *Normative Discourse.* Englewood Cliffs, N. J.: Prentice-Hall, 1961.

Watkins, Frederick M. "Natural Law and the Problem of Value Judgment." In *Political Research and Political Theory,* edited by Oliver Garceau, pp. 58-74. Cambridge, Mass.: Harvard University Press, 1968.

CHAPTER VIII

Conclusion

The student who has just read this book has found himself confronted by a conglomeration of terms and ideas, old as well as new, familiar and unfamiliar, which have been defined, redefined, explained, re-explained, elaborated and expounded, perhaps to the point of exhaustion. And yet in actual fact, neither he nor the author has done any more than scratch the proverbial surface.

Throughout the entire period of recorded history, and presumably even before that, mankind has pursued knowledge of himself, his goals, and his world as though his survival depended upon it. Today all the evidence at our disposal seems to indicate that indeed it does. Socially, politically, ecologically, and in every other way man must understand himself and his environment if he is to adapt to it and change with it while in the process of changing it—whether he does the latter wittingly or unwittingly. It is becoming increasingly clear that at the present time man is actually changing his world far faster than his knowledge of the consequences of those changes can keep pace.

In other words, man's decisions, individual as well as social or political, and especially those which have a considerable impact upon his environment and his ability to survive in it, are, in an overwhelming number of instances, being made in a non-rational if not an irrational manner. Partial evidence, deep-seated (if not

117

unconscious) personal psychological motivations, inaccurate evaluations of the decision situation—factors which are frequently tangential rather than essential to the matter at hand—have been of far greater importance in the making of decisions crucial to the survival and the everyday lifestyles of whole societies than have been well-considered, objectively weighed and measured "reasons." Instead of being rational, most of the decisions men make have been rationalized ex post facto.

For decisions to become rational, that is, made with adequate information and evaluation of the consequences, the necessary data (knowledge) must be available. This involves the operations of science—empirically and logically confirmed, tested, replicated, validated, knowledge. Where science is required, the scientific method, both rationale and process, are also required. The one implies the other. But it also implies an understanding of the limited character of all knowledge—its tentative and probabilistic, rather than certain, nature.

Decisions, therefore, should be made in full appreciation of the dangers involved and the unforeseen consequences which uncertain as well as incomplete knowledge may prevent us from grasping. Decisions cannot always be delayed until all the evidence is in, and all the consequences and the relative importance of each cannot usually be mapped out in advance. But a better understanding of the nature of knowledge and science, truth and meaning, and the process by which they are attained, can go a long way in helping to make the decision process itself a more rational undertaking. The learning process feeds into the decision process and the output of the latter acts as a corrective of the former, much as a system and its feedback mechanism operate together when they are in phase.

Thus the post-behavioralist as well as the behavioralist, the policy scientist as well as the "pure" scientist, need each other and cannot ignore the contributions as well as the legitimate demands of the other. The matter should not be viewed as a conflict between good and evil facing each other over some sort of Manichaean abyss, or as though great primeval Apollonian and Dionysian forces were battling for control of the scientist's soul. Such clichés make for interesting rhetoric and politics, but little actual accomplishment.

Instead the situation might better be viewed as a problem involving the harnessing together of different functional segments of the overall scientific undertaking—a simple division of labor for convenience sake, and to make the research process more efficient and responsible. Thus when the purist may occasionally go off on a tangent, the policy scientist might act to tug him back again—not all the way back, perhaps, but sufficiently to keep the scientific enterprise operating more effectively from time to time. Each segment, however, should preserve its own function and identity, in a sort of Yin and Yang relationship, with neither dominating the other. Or so the ideal might dictate. But then no human endeavor, not even science, can hope to attain all its operative goals. If approximate knowledge is all we can reasonably expect to obtain from human beings who happen to be scientists, to ask for harmony as well may be to engage in folly. Certainly whatever harmony may be attained will not be perfect, by any means.

It is today's student who will, in a very brief period of time, be expected to take up the responsibility of continuing the quest for knowledge in political science and who will probably find himself forced to make an attempt to resolve these as well as the many other serious problems to which he will fall heir. If the situation looks grim at the moment, especially regarding knowledge and truth, perhaps he will be able to build upon the work of scientists past and discover new solutions.

Such, at any rate, has been the purpose of this book—to help prepare him to do that very thing. All we teachers can do, from our perspective in time, is wish him luck.

Glossary

The definitions compiled here are not always those most commonly used in everyday speech. They are, rather, those which are technically the most accurate or most easily comprehensible within the context of the subject matter of this text. Where Webster's Dictionary (paperback edition)* was applicable, it was used. Otherwise, the sources referred to are those most likely to be encountered by the beginning student. All sources cited are referenced in the general bibliography by author.

AGNOSTICISM. The belief that one can know nothing of a particular subject matter, usually God, mysticism, or transcendental subjects in general.

ANALYSIS. Breaking down a whole into its component parts; the opposite of synthesis; sometimes used as a synonym for deduction.

ANALYTIC PHILOSOPHY. A type of philosophy which views all philosophical problems as problems of language—of syntax and semantics—and which concentrates on logical analysis as the principal method of philosophical inquiry. Includes Bertrand Russell, G. E. Moore, and, at one time,

---

*MacDonald, A. M., ed., *Webster's Dictionary,* new ed. (New York: Pyramid Communications, 1972).

Alfred North Whitehead. Has much in common with logical positivism.

ANALOGY. A resemblance or similarity in certain respects between things otherwise dissimilar; reasoning from apparently similar cases. (Webster)

ANOMALY. An irregularity; something that deviates from a general rule.

ATTRIBUTE. A dichotomous indicator; it is either present or absent, or can have only two values: yes or no, + or -, etc.

AXIOM. A self-evident truth; a universally received principle (Webster); an assumption which is unquestioned and serves as the basis of a deductive system from which other "truths" are inferred, as in Euclid's geometry.

BEHAVIORALISM. A variation on the term "behaviorism"; as used in political science it refers to the belief in the efficacy of the scientific method and that the behavior of human actors rather than abstract political entities (the state, etc.) should be the proper focus of political science.

CAUSATION. An influencing relationship between at least two variables in which the direction of influence is defined to be assymetrical (one-way), having a definite time sequence (the influencing variable precedes the influenced variable in time) and spatio-temporally contiguous (the two variables occur close upon one another in time and space).

CETERIS PARIBUS ASSUMPTION. "All things being equal"; the assumption that all extraneous factors impinging upon the relationship being studied have been controlled for or are not operative at the time of the study.

COGNITION. The mental process by which knowledge is apprehended or perceived (Webster); the belief about reality resulting from one's perceptions or experiences of it.

COMMONALITY (COMMON VARIANCE). A criterion used in factor analysis to determine the degree to which certain variables may be related; "that portion of the total error-free variance that correlates with the other variables" (Anderson, Watts and Wilcox).

CONCEPT. The formation in the mind of an image, notion or idea.

CONFIDENCE (LIMITS OF). In statistics, a measure of the reliability of one's findings or the range within which one may accept or reject a hypothesis or the result of any test of that hypothesis. The limits delineate the degree of error which one might be willing to tolerate in one's test results and still consider the hypothesis (or sample or correlation coefficient, etc.) acceptable.

CONCEPTUAL SCHEME. A system or pattern of interrelated concepts; may form a framework for a theory or explanation of observed events.

CONSENSUS. Overwhelming agreement; at least 75% or over.

CORRELATION. A mutual relationship or "constant conjunction"; two events occur together with considerable frequency (measurable) and are either influencing each other or are being so influenced by outside forces that they appear to be constantly (or fairly constantly) "conjoined." In statistics, it may be measured by different coefficients, depending upon the level of measurement of the test data.

CULTURE. Those patterns of beliefs, norms and values which a group or society come to share by reason of their shared experiences and interactions with their environment and with each other. (Kluckhohn)

DECISION THEORY. In political science, usually refers to the study of public policy making; for analytical purposes the field is usually divided into the following variable clusters: 1) the decision situation, 2) the decision participants, 3) the decision organization, 4) the decision process, and 5) the decision outcome. (James M. Robinson and R. Roger Majak)

DEDUCTION. In logic, the process of inferring a particular truth from a general principle. (Webster)

DIALECTIC. Pertaining to logic; according to most interpretations of Hegel, a system of logic by which two contradictory propositions give rise to new truth—thesis, antithesis, synthesis.

EMPIRICISM. The belief that all knowledge comes from the senses—from experience; the opposite of rationalism.

EPISTEMOLOGY. That branch of philosophy which deals with knowledge, knowledge theory, whether we can know anything at all, and how a valid truth claim can be distinguished from an invalid one.

ETHICS. That branch of philosophy concerned with morals or right conduct.

EXPLANATION. An answer to the question "why?"; a theory or causal hypothesis accounting for observed relationships.

FACT. A statement asserted or demonstrated to be true (Webster). In science, a fact must be demonstrated empirically and logically validated.

FACTOR. An operationalized concept of a high degree of abstraction or generality; an influencing variable.

FACTOR ANALYSIS. A complex mathematical technique by which related variables in a particular matrix may be clustered together and the number of elements in the matrix (theoretical components) reduced; "it assumes that a correlation matrix contains or is permeated by a complex configuration of shared variance that can be expressed in terms of a limited number of common factors, each of which represents a portion of the total variance" (Anderson, Watts and Wilcox). Thus, it can be a useful and efficient tool for reasoning inductively "from data to generalizations about underlying influences causing the discovered patterns [clusters]" (Rudolf Rummel).

FUNCTIONALISM. A belief that an object or system can best be defined or studied in terms of its functions, or those activities which are necessary for its maintenance or continued existence.

GAME THEORY. An abstract and deductive study of rational decision making in situations in which two or more individuals have choices to make, preferences regarding the outcomes, and some knowledge of the choices available to each other and of each other's preferences (T. C. Schelling). It usually assumes perfect knowledge or absence of knowledge, perfect rationality, and concern only for outcomes rather than means.

GENERALIZATION. A general term, theory or conclusion; a non-operationalized hypothesis or pattern of linked concepts.

HEISENBERG'S PRINCIPLE OF UNCERTAINTY. The principle that one cannot at the same time know the position of an electron and its speed; the indeterminacy of absolute knowledge of any set of conjugate variables.

HEURISTIC. Rich in implications for further observations, experiments or conceptualizations.

HYPOTHESIS. A proposition, generalization, or statement so expressed that it can be proved or disproved by the proper presentation of evidence; a generalization which can be or has been operationalized.

IDEALISM. A philosophical system that holds that only ideas are real (Hegel), that the things men perceive are attributes only, shadows of the ideal forms which alone have perfect existence (Plato), and that men can know the real world only with considerable difficulty, if at all (Kant).

IDEOLOGY. A system of ideas, beliefs, doctrines and reasons for action expressing a particular viewpoint concerning social or political reality; according to Mannheim a rationalization in support of an established political system—the opposite of utopia.

INDICATOR. A variable which refers to or indicates (operationalizes) a particular component of a theory.

INDEX. A number indicating the end result of a particular measurement procedure; a measurement derived from the effects which the object has on other objects: in this sense it is a measured indicator—e.g., the height of a tube of mercury is an index of atmospheric pressure—also used interchangeably with the term "scale" when referring to the measurement procedure per se.

INDUCTION. In logic, reasoning from particular cases to general principles. (Webster)

INFERENCE. The act of drawing a conclusion from premises; may be deductive, inductive or retroductive; usually involves prediction.

INTERSUBJECTIVITY. Consensus; the process of general agreement by which a conclusion is held to be true by all or almost all those who investigate; a surrogate for objectivity to those who believe the latter to be unattainable.

INTUITION. A perception of truth that does not involve reasoning or analysis (Webster); an insight or hunch; a "leap" to a conclusion; a guess.

ISOMORPHISM. Having the same shape; a characteristic of models which in some way mimic observed relationships among several variables; the ratios of the relationships among the variables are closely duplicated in the model; an equivalence relation.

KNOWLEDGE. Verified belief; organized, comprehended, and validated experience.

LAW. A statement expressing an order or relationship constantly observed or demonstrated to exist; a constantly recurring regularity.

LOADING. The phrasing of a question in a survey in such a manner that the answer can be predicted; "when something in the question suggests to the respondent that one particular response is more desirable than another" (Backstrom and Hursh).

LOGIC. The science and art of reasoning correctly (Webster); usually refers to basic principles and rules of reasoning elaborated by various logicians in the past; a branch of philosophy having to do with language and inference.

LOGICAL POSITIVISM. A philosophy which unites the empirical and logical traditions of earlier periods but concentrates on science, holding that philosophy is nothing more than a "department of logic" (A. J. Ayer). Originated by the "Vienna Circle" in 1923 it includes such adherents as Rudolf Carnap and the early Ludwig Wittgenstein. Has much in common with analytic philosophy since both are concerned with language and syntax. The two terms are frequently used interchangeably.

MEANING. Signification; the sense intended or derived from the context; according to logical positivists, the meaning of a concept is determined by the process by which it is verified (see *operationalism*).

MEASUREMENT. The assignment of numerals to objects or events according to some rule; the process of mapping a real object system into an abstract one.

METAPHYSICS. That branch of philosophy which investigates ultimate reality, the principles of nature and thought; thoughts about reality and thought.

METAPOLITICS. Language and thought on the language and thought of politics; a subset of metalanguage (see A. James Gregor).

METHODOLOGY. The study of the principles (rationale) and/ or procedures (techniques) of inquiry in a particular field.

MODEL. A verbal or mathematical imitation or reproduction of observed relationships on a larger or smaller scale than the original but having the same shape (*isomorphic*); a theory or explanation of the relationships observed.

MULTIVARIATE ANALYSIS. Various mathematical techniques by which three or more interrelated variables can be analyzed at the same time; as distinct from bivariate analysis.

NOMINALISM. The belief that general terms have no correspondence to reality, but are only words which men use to group together and label similar experiences for convenience.

NORM. A rule or principle of behavior considered standard in a particular social group or culture.

NORMATIVE. Having to do with norms or rules of conduct; usually refers to moral or ethical judgments of what should or should not be done; may also refer to the average, or "norm."

NUMBERS. Symbols which are used to label quantities or objects at a high level of measurement and which can therefore be manipulated mathematically.

NUMERALS. Symbols which are used to label qualities or objects at a low level of measurement and which therefore cannot be manipulated mathematically.

OPERATIONALISM. The belief that concepts have meaning only if they can be defined in terms of some physical or mental operation, and the consequences or effects of that operation perceived, measured or verified in some way.

PARADIGM. An interrelated pattern of theories, laws and facts which serve as the basis for an approach to or view of a particular problem or discipline (Kuhn); also used to refer to an ideal or most representative case.

PARANOIA. A symptom rather than a particular disease; refers to the tendency of some individuals or societies to feel persecuted, discriminated against or in mortal danger from some imagined or unknown enemy.

PHILOSOPHY. Language and thought about language and thought; traditionally the search for knowledge of ultimate reality, truth and wisdom.

POLICY SCIENCE. Applied political or social science; the concentration on immediate social and political needs rather than "pure" research.

POLITICAL ECONOMY. Economics; a term originally designed to distinguish the economy of the state or nation from that of the household.

POSITIVISM. A philosophical system originated by Auguste Comte which holds that science is the ultimate stage in the development of human history. Not to be confused with logical positivism, a twentieth century development in philosophy.

POST-BEHAVIORALISM. A movement among some political scientists to make research in political science relevant and applicable to immediate social and political problems; frequently includes a desire to politicize the profession— that is, to get the members of the political science profession, as professionals, to take positions on political issues. (David Easton, 1969)

PRAGMATISM. A school of philosophy that makes practical consequences the test of truth. (Webster)

PREDICTION. The act of foretelling a future event, frequently the result of an inference; a means of testing an hypothesis.

PROBABILITY. In statistics a ratio between the total number of occurrences of an event to the total number of trial observations; the determination of the frequency of an occurrence to be greater or less than chance.

QUALITY. A characteristic of objects at a low level of measurement.

QUANTITY. A characteristic of objects at a high level of measurement.

QUANTUM THEORY. In physics a theory originated by Max Planck to explain the discontinuous nature of energy in light; the theory that light is composed of packets (quanta) of energy rather than waves. Present day physics, however, holds that light manifests itself as both waves and quanta, depending upon how one examines it.

RATIONALISM. A system of belief which regards reason, the mind, as the sole source of knowledge; the opposite of empiricism.

RATIONALITY. The possession or due exercise of reason. (Webster)

REALISM. The belief that general terms refer to real objects, that man can know the real world.

REASON. To argue or think logically or to deduce inferences from premises; to justify belief through the presentation of evidence; the power of the mind to draw conclusions and presumably to determine truth.

RELATIVITY. A principle (Einstein's) which asserts that all phenomena occurring in the physical universe are so conditioned that it is impossible by their means to detect absolute motion or position.

RELIABILITY. Trustworthiness and objectivity of the procedures and instruments used in the research process; also refers to the credibility of the findings.

REPLICABILITY. The property of a scientific conclusion such that when the procedures by which the conclusion was arrived at are repeated, the findings themselves are reproduced.

RESPONSE SET. A defect in a questionnaire which may induce respondents to answer all or many of the questions in the same way, without regard to the meaning of the questions or the sense of the answers. Pre-testing the questionnaire will usually indicate the cause of such bias (clumsy or incomprehensible wording, sameness of questions, of answers, or of topics, etc.).

RETRODUCTION (ABDUCTION). According to Peirce, a circular type of inference utilizing both induction and deduction, by which one "guesses" at an explanation for repeated occurrence of certain events, then tests one's guess by observations of similar events.

SCALE. A system of measurement; a rule by which numerals are assigned to objects being measured; also, the measuring instrument.

SCIENCE. Knowledge verified by the scientific method; refers to both the process by which scientific knowledge is attained and the body of knowledge which results (science as process and as product).

SCIENTISM. The belief that science will achieve everything (A. Kaplan), as postulated by nineteenth century positivists.

SEMANTICS. The systematic study of the meanings of words, signs, or language.

SIMULATION. The operation of a simulator or model of a system; can be purely mathematical, involving the use of computers. Allows experimentations in the social sciences in areas not possible otherwise, as in simulating elections, wars, etc. (Pool, Abelson and Popkin). Not to be confused with gaming (involving role-playing individuals) or game theory.

SIMULTANEITY. The property attributed to two events which occur at the same time. According to Einstein such a property cannot be demonstrated to exist independently of the observer. Both observer and event are locked into the same time—space system so that someone outside that system (an independent observer) cannot verify its existence.

SOCIALIZATION. Process of adaptation to a social environment.

SOCIOLOGY OF KNOWLEDGE. According to Mannheim the view that all beliefs (cognitions, knowledge) are determined by the interests and social situations of the believers; i.e., they are "relational" or socially determined and, therefore, universal agreement or absolute objectivity is unobtainable.

STATISTICS. A branch of mathematics which summarizes information in such a manner as to make it more usable, and tests generalizations or inductive inferences about populations on the basis of probability samples; the principal tool of inductive statistics is probability theory.

STRUCTURALISM. The belief that the structure of the brain determines the perception and conception of reality and the process by which knowledge is attained; that the brain may and does frequently distort or destroy incoming data so that cognitions may be inaccurately apprehended.

SYLLOGISM. A logical form of argument consisting of three propositions; a major and a minor premise and a conclusion which follows from and is implied in the first two; the truth of the conclusion depends upon the truth of the major and minor premises.

SYNTAX. Rules of grammar governing the arrangement of words in a sentence.

SYNTHESIS. The combination of separate elements into a whole; the opposite of analysis; sometimes used as a synonym for induction.

SYSTEM. A whole composed of parts working together to perform a particular function or set of functions.

TAUTOLOGY. A statement which tells us nothing about the real world because it is always true and can be nothing but true; e.g., "Tomorrow it will either rain or it will not."

THEORY. An explanation of any set of relationships observed; a confirmed hypothesis.

TRUTH. Property of a statement which has been verified as being in agreement with reality.

UNIVERSAL. A general term applying to all members of a particular class.

UTOPIA. According to Mannheim a system of political ideas which rationalizes and urges action on behalf of the reform of or revolution against an existing political system; the opposite of ideology.

VALIDITY. In logic, the result of a deductive exercise—i.e., a conclusion is valid if it can be logically deduced from two general premises; in empirical research, refers to the property of the research instrument when it accurately measures what it was intended to measure.

VALUE. A thing of worth, of importance; a need or interest.

VALUE JUDGMENT. A choice, decision or determination of preference.

VALUE THEORY. A set of guidelines for the analysis of the meaning and justification for the holding of values.

VARIABLE. A component of a theory; a concept which has been operationalized.

VERIFICATION. The process of confirming the truth of a statement by the presentation of empirical evidence; includes the criteria validity, reliability and replicability.

Bibliography

Ackerman, Robert. *Theories of Knowledge: A Critical Introduction.* New York: McGraw-Hill, 1965.

Alker, Hayward R., Jr. *Mathematics and Politics.* New York: Macmillan, 1965.

Anderson, Lee F., Meredith W. Watts, and Allen R. Wilcox. *Legislative Roll-Call Analysis.* Evanston, Ill.: Northwestern University Press, 1966.

Apter, David E., ed. *Ideology and Discontent.* New York: The Free Press of Glencoe, 1964.

———, and Charles F. Andrain, eds. *Contemporary Analytical Theory.* Englewood Cliffs, N. J.: Prentice-Hall, 1972.

Ayer, A. J., ed. *Logical Positivism.* Glencoe, Ill.: The Free Press, 1959.

———. "Verification and Experience." In *Logical Positivism,* edited by A. J. Ayer, pp. 228-43. Glencoe, Ill.: The Free Press, 1959.

———, and Raymond Winch, eds. *British Empirical Philosophers: Locke, Berkeley, Hume, Reid and J. S. Mill.* New York: Simon and Schuster, A Clarion Book, 1968.

Backstrom, Charles H., and Gerald D. Hursh. *Survey Research.* Evanston, Ill.: Northwestern University Press, 1963.

Baker, Kendall L., Sami J. Hajjar, and Alan Evan Schenker. "Note on Behavioralists and Post-behavioralists in Contemporary Political Science." *P.S.* 5 (Summer, 1972): 271-73.

Ball, Howard and Thomas P. Lauth, Jr. *Changing Perspectives in Contemporary Political Analysis: Readings on the Dimensions of Scientific and Political Inquiry.* Englewood Cliffs, N. J.: Prentice-Hall, 1971.

Barbour, Ian G. *Issues in Science and Religion.* Englewood Cliffs, N. J.: Prentice-Hall, 1966.

Barker, S. F. *The Elements of Logic.* New York: McGraw-Hill, 1965.

Bauer, Raymond A. *Social Indicators.* Cambridge, Mass.: M.I.T. Press, 1966.

Becker, Howard and Harry Elmer Barnes. *Social Thought From Lore to Science.* 3d ed. 3 vols. New York: Dover, 1961.

Bentley, Arthur F. *The Process of Government.* Cambridge, Mass.: Harvard University Press, 1967.

Blalock, Hubert M., Jr. *Causal Inferences in Nonexperimental Research.* Chapel Hill: University of North Carolina Press, 1964.

Blalock, Hubert M., Jr. *An Introduction to Social Research.* Englewood Cliffs, N. J.: Prentice-Hall, 1970.

―――. *Social Statistics.* New York: McGraw-Hill, 1960.

―――. *Theory Construction: From Verbal to Mathematical Formulations.* Englewood Cliffs, N. J.: Prentice-Hall, 1969.

―――, and Ann B. Blalock, eds. *Methodology in Social Research.* New York: McGraw-Hill, 1968.

Brecht, Arnold. *Political Theory: The Foundations of Twentieth Century Political Thought.* Princeton, N. J.: Princeton University Press, 1959.

Bluhm, William T. *Theories of the Political System.* 2d ed. Englewood Cliffs, N. J.: Prentice-Hall, 1971.

Braithwaite, Richard Bevan. *Scientific Explanation.* New York: Harper and Row, 1960.

Braybrooke, David and Alexander Rosenberg. "Comment: Getting the War News Straight: The Actual Situation in the Philosophy of Science." *APSR* 66 (September 1972): 818-26.

Bridgman, Percy W. *The Logic of Modern Physics.* New York: Macmillan, 1927.

Brodbeck, May, ed. *Readings in the Philosophy of the Social Sciences.* New York: Macmillan, 1968.

Bronowski, Jacob. *The Common Sense of Science.* Cambridge, Mass.: Harvard University Press, 1958.

―――. *Science and Human Values.* Rev. ed. New York: Harper and Row, 1965.

Buchanan, William. *Understanding Political Variables.* New York: Charles Scribner's Sons, 1969.

Canfield, John V. and Franklin H. Donnell, Jr., eds. *Readings in the Theory of Knowledge.* New York: Appleton-Century-Crofts, 1964.

Cassirer, Ernst. *The Problem of Knowledge.* New Haven: Yale University Press, 1950.

Charlesworth, James C., ed. *Contemporary Political Analysis.* New York: The Free Press, 1967.

―――, ed. *A Design for Political Science: Scope, Objectives and Methods.* Philadelphia: The American Academy of Political and Social Science, December 1966.

―――, ed. *The Limits of Behavioralism in Political Science.* Philadelphia: The American Academy of Political and Social Science, October 1962.

Cohen, Morris Raphael. *A Preface to Logic.* New York: Meridian Books, 1956.

―――. *Reason and Nature: The Meaning of Scientific Method.* 2d ed. New York: The Free Press of Glencoe, 1964.

――― and Ernest Nagel. *An Introduction to Logic and Scientific Method.* New York: Harcourt, Brace and Company, 1934.

Coleman, James S. *Introduction to Mathematical Sociology.* New York: The Free Press of Glencoe, 1964.

Conant, James B. *Science and Common Sense.* New Haven: Yale University Press, 1951.

Connolly, William E. *Political Science and Ideology.* New York: Atherton Press, 1967.

Crick, Bernard. *The American Science of Politics: Its Origins and Conditions.* Berkeley and Los Angeles: University of California Press, 1960.

―――. *In Defence of Politics.* Chicago: University of Chicago Press, 1962.

Dahl, Robert A. "The Behavioral Approach in Political Science: Epitaph for a Monument to a Successful Protest." *APSR* 55 (December 1961): 763-72.

―――. *Modern Political Analysis.* Englewood Cliffs, N. J.: Prentice-Hall, 1963.

―――, and Deane E. Neubauer, eds. *Readings in Modern Political Analysis.* Englewood Cliffs, N. J.: Prentice-Hall, 1968.

de Sola Pool, Ithiel, ed. *Contemporary Political Science: Toward Empirical Theory.* New York: McGraw-Hill, 1967.

Dewey, John. *Logic: The Theory of Inquiry.* New York: Holt, Rinehart and Winston, 1938.

―――. *The Quest for Certainty: A Study of the Relation of Knowledge and Action.* New York: G. P. Putnam's Sons, Capricorn

Books edition, 1960.

Diesing, Paul. *Patterns of Discovery in the Social Sciences.* Chicago: Aldine-Atherton, 1971.

Duverger, Maurice. *An Introduction to the Social Sciences.* New York: Praeger, 1964.

Dye, Thomas R. *Understanding Public Policy.* Englewood Cliffs, N. J.: Prentice-Hall, 1972.

Easton, David. "The New Revolution in Political Science." *APSR* 63 (December 1969): 1051-61.

―――. *The Political System.* 2d ed. New York: Knopf, 1971.

Eddington, Sir Arthur. *The Nature of the Physical World.* Ann Arbor: University of Michigan Press, 1958.

Einstein, Albert. *Relativity, The Special and General Theory: A Popular Exposition.* Translated by Robert W. Lawson. New York: Crown Publishers, 1961.

Eulau, Heinz. *The Behavioral Persuasion in Politics.* New York: Random House, 1963.

―――, ed. *Behavioralism in Political Science.* New York: Atherton Press, 1969.

―――, Samuel J. Eldersveld and Morris Janowitz, eds. *Political Behavior.* Glencoe, Ill.: The Free Press, 1956.

――― and James G. March, eds. *Political Science: The Behavioral and Social Sciences Survey, Political Science Panel.* Englewood Cliffs, N. J.: Prentice-Hall, A Spectrum Book, 1969.

Feigl, Herbert, and May Brodbeck, eds. *Readings in the Philosophy of Science.* New York: Appleton-Century-Crofts, 1953.

Festinger, Leon and Daniel Katz, eds. *Research Methods in the Behavioral Sciences.* New York: Holt, Rinehart and Winston, 1953.

Flathman, Richard E. *The Public Interest: An Essay Concerning the Normative Discourse of Politics.* New York: John Wiley and Sons, 1966.

Fox, Charles J. "Democratic Elitism Close to Home." *P.S.* 4 (Spring 1971): 126-29.

Frank, Philipp. *The Philosophy of Science.* Englewood Cliffs, N. J.: Prentice-Hall, 1957.

Fredrich, Carl J., ed. *The Philosophy of Hegel.* New York: Random House, The Modern Library, 1954.

Frohock, Fred M. *The Nature of Political Inquiry.* Homewood, Ill.: Dorsey Press, 1967.

Galtung, Johan. *Theory and Methods of Social Research.* New York: Columbia University Press, 1967.

Gamow, George. *Thirty Years That Shook Physics, The Story of Quantum Theory*. Garden City, N. Y.: Doubleday, Anchor Books, 1966.

Garceau, Oliver, ed. *Political Research and Political Theory*. Cambridge, Mass.: Harvard University Press, 1968.

Golembiewski, Robert T., William A. Welsh and William J. Crotty. *A Methodological Primer for Political Scientists*. Chicago: Rand McNally, 1969.

Gould, James A., and Vincent V. Thursby, eds. *Contemporary Political Thought: Issues in Scope, Value and Direction*. New York: Holt, Rinehart and Winston, 1969.

Greer, Scott. *The Logic of Social Inquiry*. Chicago: Aldine, 1969.

Gregor, A. James. *An Introduction to Metapolitics: A Brief Inquiry into the Conceptual Language of Political Science*. New York: The Free Press, 1971.

Haas, Michael and Theodore L. Becker. "A Multimethodological Plea." *Polity* 2 (Spring 1970): 267-94.

Haas, Michael, and Henry S. Kariel, eds. *Approaches to the Study of Political Science*. Scranton, Pa.: Chandler, 1970.

Hacker, Andrew. *Political Theory: Philosophy, Ideology, Science*. New York: Macmillan, 1961.

Hallowell, John H. *Main Currents in Modern Political Thought*. New York: Henry Holt and Company, 1950.

Hanson, Norwood Russell. *Patterns of Discovery*. Cambridge: Harvard University Press, 1965.

Hayakawa, S. I. *Language in Thought and Action*. 3d ed. New York: Harcourt, Brace & World, 1972.

Hayes, Louis D., and Ronald D. Hedlund, eds. *The Conduct of Political Inquiry*. Englewood Cliffs, N. J.: Prentice-Hall, 1970.

Hempel, Carl G. *Aspects of Scientific Explanation*. New York: The Free Press, 1965.

―――. *The Philosophy of Natural Science*. Englewood Cliffs, N. J.: Prentice-Hall, 1966.

Holsti, Ole R. *Content Analysis for The Social Sciences and The Humanities*. Reading, Mass.: Addison-Wesley, 1969.

Homans, George C. *The Nature of Social Science*. New York: Harcourt, Brace and World, 1967.

Hospers, John. *Introduction to Philosophical Analysis*. 2d ed. Englewood Cliffs, N. J.: Prentice-Hall, 1967.

Hume, David. *Inquiry Concerning Human Understanding*. Edited by L. A. Selby-Bigge. Oxford: Clarendon Press, 1894.

Isaak, Alan C. *Scope and Methods of Political Science.* Homewood, Ill.: Dorsey Press, 1969.

Kalleberg, Arthur L. "Concept Formation in Normative and Empirical Studies: Toward Reconciliation in Political Theory." *APSR* 63 (March 1969): 26-93.

Kant, Immanuel. *Critique of Practical Reason.* Translated and introduced by Lewis White Beck. New York: Bobbs-Merrill, Liberal Arts Press, 1956.

————. *Critique of Pure Reason.* 2d ed. Translated by F. Max Muller. Garden City, N. Y.: Doubleday, Anchor Books, 1961.

Kaplan, Abraham. *The Conduct of Inquiry.* San Francisco: Chandler, 1964.

————. *The New World of Philosophy.* New York: Vintage Books, 1961.

Kemeny, John G. *A Philosopher Looks At Science.* New York: Van Nostrand and Reinhold, 1959.

Kerlinger, Fred. *Foundations of Behavioral Research.* New York: Holt, Rinehart and Winston, 1964.

Key, V. O., Jr. *A Primer of Statistics for Political Scientists.* Foreword by Frank Munger. New York: Crowell, 1966.

Kluckhohn, Clyde. *Culture and Behavior.* Edited by Richard Kluckhohn. New York: The Free Press, 1962.

Kroeber, A. L., and Clyde Kluckhohn. *Culture.* New York: Vintage Books, 1963.

Kuhn, Thomas S. *The Structure of Scientific Revolutions.* Chicago: University of Chicago Press, 1962.

Kyburg, Henry E., Jr. *Probability and Inductive Logic.* London: Macmillan, 1970.

Landau, Martin. "Comment: On Objectivity." *APSR* 66 (September 1972): 846-56.

————. *Political Theory and Political Science: Studies in the Methodology of Political Inquiry.* New York: Macmillan, 1972.

Lasswell, Harold D. *The Future of Political Science.* New York: Prentice-Hall, Atherton Press, 1963.

————. *Politics: Who Gets What, When, How.* Re-issued by Meridian Books, New York, 1958.

————, and Abraham Kaplan. *Power and Society.* New Haven: Yale University Press, 1950.

Lazarsfeld, Paul F., and Neil W. Henry, eds. *Readings in Mathematical Social Science.* Cambridge: M.I.T. Press, 1968.

————, and Morris Rosenberg, eds. *The Language of Social Re-*

search, *A Reader in the Methodology of Social Research.* New York: The Free Press, 1965.

Lerner, Daniel, ed. *Cause and Effect, The Hayden Colloquium on Scientific Method and Concept.* New York: The Free Press, 1965.

———, ed. *Evidence and Inference, The Hayden Colloquium on Scientific Method and Concept.* Glencoe, Ill.: The Free Press, 1959.

———, ed. *The Human Meaning of the Social Sciences.* Cleveland, Ohio: World Publishing Company, 1959.

———, ed. *Quantity and Quality, The Hayden Colloquium on Scientific Method and Concept.* New York: The Free Press of Glencoe, 1961.

———, and Harold D. Lasswell, eds. *The Policy Sciences.* Stanford, Calif.: Stanford University Press, 1951.

Lipset, Seymour Martin, ed. *Politics and the Social Sciences.* New York: Oxford University Press, 1969.

Locke, John. *An Essay Concerning Human Understanding.* 2 vols. Edited by Alexander Campbell Fraser. Oxford: Clarendon Press, 1894. Abridged edition edited by Russell Kirk. Chicago: Henry Regnery Co., Gateway Editions, 1956.

Lynd, Robert S. *Knowledge for What?* New York: Grove Press, 1964. First published by Princeton University Press, 1939.

Macdonald, A. M., ed. *Webster's Dictionary, New Edition.* New York: Pyramid Communications, 1972.

Mannheim, Karl. *Ideology and Utopia: An Introduction to the Sociology of Knowledge.* Translated by Louis Wirth and Edward Shils. New York: Harcourt, Brace and World, Harvest Books, 1936.

McCoy, Charles A., and John Playford. *Apolitical Politics, A Critique of Behavioralism.* New York: Thomas Y. Crowell, 1967.

Meehan, Eugene J. *Explanation in Social Science: A System Paradigm.* Homewood, Ill.: Dorsey Press, 1968.

———. *The Foundations of Political Analysis, Empirical and Normative.* Homewood, Ill.: Dorsey Press, 1971.

———. *The Theory and Method of Political Analysis.* Homewood, Ill.: Dorsey Press, 1965.

———. *Value Judgment and Social Science.* Homewood, Ill.: Dorsey Press, 1969.

Merton, Robert K. *Social Theory and Social Structure.* Rev. ed. New York: The Free Press, 1957.

Mill, John Stuart. *Philosophy of Scientific Method.* New York: Hafner, 1950.

Miller, Eugene F. "Positivism, Historicism and Political Inquiry." *APSR* 66 (September, 1972): 796-819.

————. "Rejoinder to 'Comments' by David Braybrooke and Alexander Rosenberg, Richard S. Rudner and Martin Landau." *APSR* 66 (September 1972): 857-730.

Murphy, Joseph S. *Political Theory, A Conceptual Analysis.* Homewood, Ill.: Dorsey Press, 1968.

Myrdal, Gunnar. *Objectivity in Social Research.* New York: Pantheon, Random House, 1969.

Nagel, Ernest. *The Structure of Science.* New York: Harcourt, Brace and World, 1961.

Natanson, Maurice. *The Philosophy of The Social Sciences: A Reader.* New York: Random House, 1963.

Northrup, F.S.C. *The Logic of the Sciences and the Humanities.* Cleveland, Ohio: World Publishing Company, 1959.

Obler, Paul C., and Herman A. Estrin, eds. *The New Scientist: Essays in the Methods and Values of Modern Science.* Garden City, N. Y.: Doubleday and Company, Anchor Books, 1962.

Osgood, Charles E., George J. Suci, and Percy H. Tannenbaum. *The Measurement of Meaning.* Urbana: University of Illinois Press, 1957.

Palter, Robert M. *Whitehead's Philosophy of Science.* Chicago: University of Chicago Press, 1960.

Pap, Arthur. *An Introduction to the Philosophy of Science.* New York: The Free Press, 1962.

Pico della Mirandola, Giovanni. *Oration on the Dignity of Man.* Translated by A. Robert Caponigri. Chicago: Henry Regnery Co., Gateway Edition, 1956.

Poincaré, Henry. *Science and Hypothesis.* Translated by G. B. Halstead. New York: The Science Press, 1905.

Polanyi, Michael. *Personal Knowledge.* Chicago: University of Chicago Press, 1958.

Polsby, Nelson W., Robert A. Dentler and Paul A. Smith, eds. *Politics and Social Life.* Boston: Houghton-Mifflin, 1963.

Pool, Ithiel de Sola, Robert P. Abelson, and Samuel Popkin. *Candidates, Issues and Strategies.* Rev. ed. Cambridge, Mass.: M.I.T. Press, 1965.

Popper, Karl R. *The Logic of Scientific Discovery.* Rev. ed. New York: Harper and Row, 1965.

———. *The Poverty of Historicism.* New York: Harper and Row, Torchbook edition, 1964.

Quine, W. V. *Word and Object.* New York: John Wiley and Sons, 1960.

Ranney, Austin, ed. *Essays on the Behavioral Study of Politics.* Urbana: University of Illinois Press, 1962.

———, ed. *Political Science and Public Policy.* Sponsored by the Committee on Governmental and Legal Processes of the Social Science Research Council. Chicago: Markham, 1968.

Reichenbach, Hans. *Modern Philosophy of Science.* Translated and edited by Maria Reichenbach. London: Routledge and Kegan Paul, 1959.

———. *Elements of Symbolic Logic.* New York: The Free Press, 1966.

———. *The Rise of Scientific Philosophy.* Berkeley and Los Angeles: University of California Press, 1951.

Rosenblueth, Arturo. *Mind and Brain: A Philosophy of Science.* Cambridge: M.I.T. Press, 1970.

Rudner, Richard S. "Comment: On Evolving Standard Views in Philosophy of Science." *APSR* 66 (September 1972): 827-45.

———. *The Philosophy of Social Science.* Englewood Cliffs, N. J.: Prentice-Hall, 1966.

Rummel, Rudolf J. *Applied Factor Analysis.* Evanston, Ill.: Northwestern University Press, 1970.

Runciman, W. G. *Social Science and Political Theory.* Cambridge: Cambridge University Press, 1963.

Russell, Bertrand. *A History of Western Philosophy.* New York: Simon and Schuster, 1945.

———. *An Inquiry into Meaning and Truth.* Baltimore, Md.: Penguin Books, 1962.

———. *The Scientific Outlook.* New York: W. W. Norton, 1931, renewed 1959.

Sabine, George H. *A History of Political Theory.* New York: Henry Holt and Company, 1950.

de Santillana, Giorgio. *The Origins of Scientific Thought, from Anaximander to Proclus, 600 B.C. - 500 A.D.* Chicago: University of Chicago Press, 1961.

Schaar, John H., and Sheldon S. Wolin. "Essays on the Scientific Study of Politics: A Critique." *APSR* 57 (March, 1963): 125-50.

Scheffler, Israel. *Science and Subjectivity.* Indianapolis: Bobbs-Merrill, 1967.

Schilpp, Paul Arthur. *The Philosophy of Rudolf Carnap.* La Salle, Ill.: Open Court, 1963.

Shklar, Judith N., ed. *Political Theory and Ideology.* New York: Macmillan, 1966.

Sjoberg Gideon. *Ethics, Politics and Social Research.* Cambridge, Mass.: Schenckman, 1967.

———, and Roger Nett. *A Methodology for Social Research.* New York: Harper and Row, 1968.

Skinner, B. F. *Science and Human Behavior.* New York: The Free Press, 1965.

Somit, Albert and Joseph Tanenhaus. *American Political Science, A Profile of a Discipline.* New York: Prentice-Hall, Atherton Press, 1964.

———. *The Development of Political Science.* Boston: Allyn and Bacon, 1967.

Stark, W. *The Sociology of Knowledge: An Essay in Aid of a Deeper Understanding of the History of Ideas.* London: Routledge and Kegan Paul, 1958.

Storing, Herbert J., ed. *Essays on the Scientific Study of Politics.* New York: Holt, Rinehart and Winston, 1962.

Taylor, Paul W. *Normative Discourse.* Englewood Cliffs, N. J.: Prentice-Hall, 1961.

Thompson, Manley. *The Pragmatic Philosophy of C. S. Peirce.* Chicago: University of Chicago Press, Phoenix Books, 1963.

Torgerson, Warren S. *Theory and Methods of Scaling.* New York: John Wiley and Sons, 1958.

Toulmin, Stephen. *Foresight and Understanding: An Enquiry into the Aims of Science.* Foreword by Jacques Barzun. New York: Harper and Row, Torchbook edition, 1963.

———. *The Philosophy of Science: An Introduction.* New York: Harper and Row, 1960.

Truman, David. *The Governmental Process.* New York: Knopf, 1951.

Turner, Merle B. *Philosophy and the Science of Behavior.* New York: Appleton-Century-Crofts, 1967.

Ulmer, S. Sidney. *Introductory Readings in Political Behavior.* Chicago: Rand McNally, 1961.

Van Dyke, Vernon. *Political Science: A Philosophical Analysis.* Stanford, Calif.: Stanford University Press, 1960.

Voegelin, Eric. *The New Science of Politics, An Introduction.* Chicago: University of Chicago Press, 1952.

Weber, Max. *Methodology of the Social Sciences.* Translated and edited by Edward A. Shils and Henry A. Finch, with a foreword by Edward A. Shils. Glencoe, Ill.: The Free Press, 1949.

Weldon, T. D. *Vocabulary of Politics.* London: Pelican Books, 1953.

White, Morton. *The Age of Analysis.* New York: Mentor Books, New American Library, 1955.

Whitehead, Alfred North. *Modes of Thought.* New York: The Free Press, 1968.

Winch, Peter. *The Idea of a Social Science: And Its Relation to Philosophy.* London: Routledge and Kegan Paul, 1958.

Wittgenstein, Ludwig. *Philosophical Investigations.* Translated by G. E. M. Anscombe. Oxford: Basil Blackwell, 1953.

———. *Tractatus Logico-Philosophicus.* London: Routledge and Kegan Paul, 1922.

Wolff, Kurt H., ed. *From Karl Mannheim.* New York: Oxford University Press, 1971.

Wolin, Sheldon S. *Politics and Vision.* Boston: Little, Brown and Company, 1960.

Index